Monks Rest, Littleton: probably a medieval priest's house first recognised and described by Ken Roberts, our friend and co-author who died on March 23rd 1987 and to whom this volume is dedicated.

MEDIEVAL HALL HOUSES
OF THE WINCHESTER AREA

Winchester City Museum

MEDIEVAL HALL HOUSES
OF THE WINCHESTER AREA

by Elizabeth Lewis, Edward Roberts
and Kenneth Roberts

Drawings by Nigel Fradgley

Copyright © 1988 Mid Hampshire Buildings Survey Group

Photographs by John Bosworth (JRB) John Crook (PMJC), Eric Lane (EL), The Hampshire Chronicle (HC), Winchester City Museum (WCM), and Edward Roberts (EVR)

The drawings of The Curio Shop, Wickham, are reproduced by permission of the Hampshire Field Club and Archaeological Society

Design and layout by Susan Hudson

Typesetting by David Eno

Printed by Gabare, Winchester

Bound by R. Harsher

Published by Winchester City Museum

ISBN 0 86135 011 1

Acknowledgements

Our grateful thanks are due to all the owners of the houses listed, who have borne with a great deal of disruption, measuring and sometimes heated argument while survey was in progress; to the Marc Fitch Fund, to Hampshire County Council and King Alfred's College, Winchester for their generous grants towards the preparation of drawings and the printing of the volume; to the Hampshire Field Club Historic Buildings Section for enabling us to publish the frontispiece as a memorial to Ken Roberts who was a founder member of the Section and our co-author; to Peter Smith, Eric Mercer and Jim Oliver for their valuable advice and comments on the text and for their sustained encouragement while the book was in progress; to Anne Bannister and Colin Byers, Gerry and Leslie Blake, Mara Buchanan Jones, Ken and Pat Hagyard, Trevor and Sue Harvey and Freddie Stanfield for their practical help; to Mavis Foyster and Judith Blake for their skill in preparing the text and lastly to Connie Roberts for her humour, patience and support throughout the work.

Contents

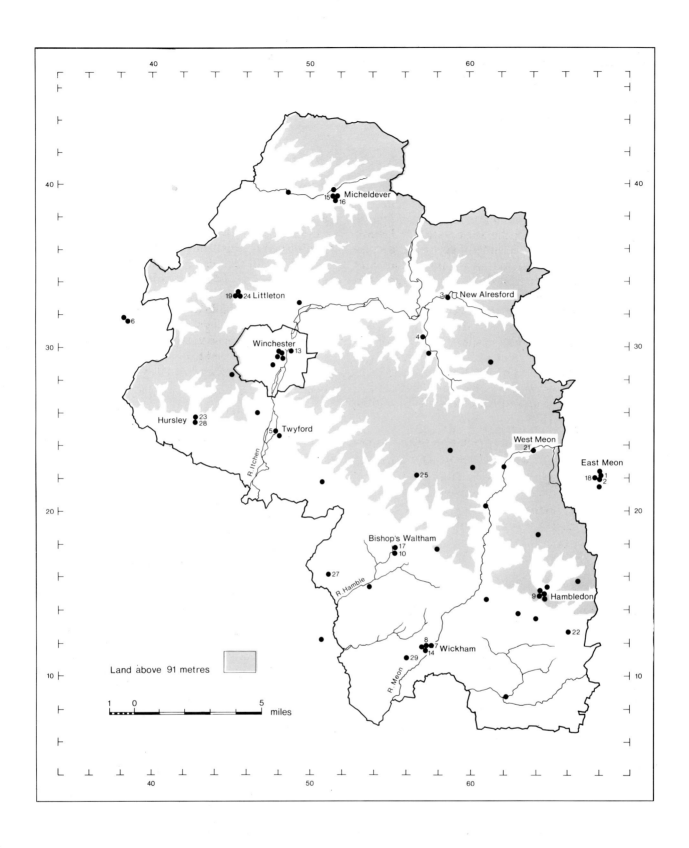

Fig. 1 The landscape of central Hampshire showing the location
of buildings in the text and gazeteer

10

Introduction

This book is intended as an introduction and guide for those concerned with the conservation and repair of small medieval buildings (often the owner-occupiers themselves) and also as a quarry of building types for specialists seeking comparisons with the houses of other regions. Our aim is to explore the evidence for the houses as they were originally built, and in our drawings we have therefore underplayed or omitted completely any later features and alterations, however interesting in themselves. We hope on some future occasion to rectify the balance by presenting our views of post-medieval houses and the post-medieval up-grading of medieval ones.[1]

The buildings shown here are selected from perhaps seventy examples seen in some ten years of observation. They are those in which the original structure is fairly complete and where we can be reasonably confident about our interpretation; but the future discovery of previously concealed evidence or alternative reading of the existing evidence is always possible and we welcome debate.

The date range of the houses discussed starts in the fourteenth century and ends in the mid sixteenth. This period spans the development and decline of the medieval hall house, which we take as our theme.

In the matter of detailed chronology our suggestions are tentative. For the houses we have selected, such documents as survive do not provide reliable dating evidence and no timber samples were available for dendrochronology (tree ring dating). The sequence we suggest is based upon the development of forms elsewhere in the country or as implied by constructional details.

The area from which our examples are drawn is centred on Winchester and the parishes mainly to the south-east which are now part of the district administered by the City of Winchester. Geographically this includes the upper reaches of the rivers Itchen, Hamble and Meon whose gravelly valley deposits overlie the upper chalk, the dominant geology of the area, and one that has influenced the landscape, the economy and the available building materials. Village settlements tend to be concentrated along the river valleys, with more isolated hamlets and farms on the downs. The three largest settlements outside Winchester are the small towns of New Alresford, Bishop's Waltham

and Wickham. Of these Wickham may be late Saxon in origin, while New Alresford was a new town established by the Bishop of Winchester (Beresford 1959, 187-215) and Bishop's Waltham was probably another. Several of the houses described here occupy prime sites in planned street layouts, but even the earliest (for example at East Meon) are probably replacement buildings. The houses of Winchester itself have been recorded by others (Keene 1985, 156-180), and are referred to here mainly as a contrast in design between urban and village houses.

The medieval houses described here were occupied by men and women from the middle rank of society. They were in the main peasant farmers who, in the Winchester area, generally held their land of some great ecclesiastical landlord. Although the term 'peasant' may serve for the 14th and 15th centuries (Dyer 1986,21) yet the evidence of early inventories (discussed in Part 2) suggests that in the 16th century they would most probably have considered themselves prosperous husbandmen, or yeomen. More accurately, we should say that these houses were occupied by people of equivalent wealth or status to the yeoman class. At least one, Monk's Rest at Littleton (24), may have been the home of a village priest, while others were probably the homes of moderately well-to-do craftsmen. On either side of these people of middle rank were those whose houses have been excluded from consideration by necessity or choice. The hovels of the poor have not survived; the houses of the rich, from the great landlord to the country gentleman, were on a different scale from the yeoman's hall and deserve separate study.

The design of hall houses varied considerably but the essential component was always there, the hall itself. The hall was open from floor to rafters. Thus smoke from the fire burning on the hearth could rise unhindered to escape through a louvre or gablet in the roof. The hall floor was generally of beaten earth, or stone, without floor boards[2]. Other rooms in the house were generally built on two floors. In our area, the smaller hall house was timber-framed, that is made from timbers which were jointed together to form a wooden skeleton which was infilled with wattle and daub. This timber structure was divided into bays by cross frames and roof trusses. The terms used to describe the different members of this timber framing are given in the illustrated glossary on pages 00-00.

---

[1] Field surveys, photographs and detailed notes to the buildings are held at Winchester City Museum.

[2] In the following text, we refer to the flooring of the hall, a verbal convention meaning the insertion of joists to support the floor of a chamber above the hall.

Cripstead Farmhouse, Back Street, St. Cross (60). A single bay hall and service range with contemporary cross wing. (WCM)

The grander halls of wealthy landlords were divided into two or more bays by an open truss where carpentry skill and quality timber could best be displayed. It was here that the lord could receive his friends, eat ceremoniously and settle legal matters with his tenants and neighbours. Social distinction was implicit in its very design. The 'high' end where the lord and his family sat was distinguished by a raised dias, or by a canopy. In the smaller buildings which we describe, social distinctions of a humbler sort were similarly observed. For the yeoman and his family seated at the high end of his hall, the equivalent of the lord's canopy was a covered area formed by an overshot chamber above – as, for example, at Park View, Tichborne (4), or a finely moulded dais beam – as at Monks Rest Littleton (24).

A door from the high end of the hall led to the private quarters of the family. This was a floored bay with a chamber above which was often well finished with chamfered timbers. Occasionally, as at Littleton Manor (19) or The Crease (16), we find an arch-braced truss over the chamber above the parlour. At the low end of the hall there was usually a passage connecting two opposing doors that led into the building. Beyond the passage was another bay, usually floored; this ground floor bay for the domestic services and preparation of food was occasionally divided into two with separate access to each via the passage, as at 78 Hursley (23) or Preshaw Farm Cottages (25), where both service doorways survive. At The Crease a further doorway provided access to stairs leading up to the first floor. We have no examples in these small houses of a central passage leading to the kitchen (presumably a separate building) which is a feature of large halls such as that at St Cross hospital near Winchester (although here the alignment of the kitchen to the hall is not typical). Not all houses boast two floored bays; Forge Sound (1) and Embassy Cottage (5) have only one, apparently from the beginning.

This then was the pattern for small halls in Hampshire and in the main it is very close to the plan form elsewhere in the country; it is in the detail that Hampshire asserts its own vernacular tradition.

Part One

The Development of the Medieval Hall in Hampshire

Aisled and quasi aisled halls

There are some standing buildings in our area predating the fourteenth century, these are stone built first floor halls and represent a separate building tradition from the timber-framed structures we shall be dealing with. The two traditions may well have been combined in some instances; for example at Hambledon Manor (43) where a surviving two-floored stone building appears to be a cross-wing communicating by three stone doorways on the ground floor with hall, possibly of timber, now vanished. A similar arrangement may have existed at St. Clair's Farm, Soberton (62) where a fine first floor hall survives in isolation. At Rookwood Farm, Denmead (37) a classic Norman first floor hall appears to be virtually complete, comparable with the examples at Southampton and Christchurch. The evolution of building design in the twelfth and thirteenth century is still known mainly from archaeological evidence outside Hampshire or from fragmentary surviving buildings such as these, in the higher social bracket; smaller houses are virtually unknown.

Farnham Castle, dated by Cecil Hewett (1980, 39) to between 1115 and 1145 is one of the earliest.

The aisled structure was a device to span a wide space and was appropriate for large buildings such as churches, barns and palatial halls. Perhaps therefore we should not expect to see it in halls of lesser consequence than those of kings and bishops. However, throughout the Middle Ages building fashion as set by the wealthy or aristocratic landowner was an important model to the lower ranks of society. The dominance of the see of Winchester was fundamental both in terms of land ownership and in the diffusion of up-to-date building types which must have provided models for other builders in the area. At East Meon there are two halls standing opposite each other across what must be an abandoned medieval street. Both have a single aisle on the side of the house away from the street. Forge Sound (1) is aisled throughout, with a hall 14ft wide and an aisle 3ft 9ins wide. The hall truss has a tie beam supported by arch braces and jowled posts and the roof has common rafters, each pair joined by collars which have lapped dovetail joints.

Two early medieval houses at East Meon. Forge Sound is the single aisled house on the left, facing Riverside (centre) with its sixteenth century annexe on the right. (PMJC)

The aisled hall seems to be the first identifiable type to succeed the upper floor hall; but as mentioned above, it may well have co-existed with the stone-built floored block. The impact of Henry III's great aisled hall at Winchester Castle (dated between 1225 and 1235) must have been very powerful locally and copied more extensively than surviving examples suggest: the aisled hall at Warnford built by the St. John family may be broadly contemporary (Wood 1965, 11: Nisbett 1906, 299-307).

Standing examples of timber-framed aisled halls are still relatively uncommon, though being recognised in increasing numbers, particularly in the south east of Britain. The bishop of Winchester's hall at

There is none of the scissor bracing that is often associated with the aisled form elsewhere, although the wall framing of the cross frames and the front wall shows a predilection for very long braces and large open panels which suggests an early date.

Riverside (2), opposite, has similar wall framing and the parlour and service bays are both aisled, but the hall itself is constructed in the new mode, with a single base cruck, a large curved timber which bridges the aisle and supports the arcade plate, thus removing the need for an arcade post in the hall.

Halls built with base crucks were generally large and of high status, and even locally there are splendid

ALCOCK 1981

HAMPSHIRE VARIATIONS

Full crucks

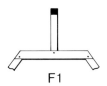

F1

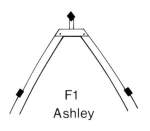

F1
Ashley

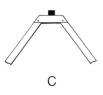

C

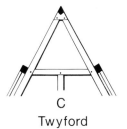

C
Twyford

E

E
Rockbourne

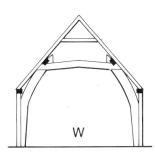

W

Base cruck

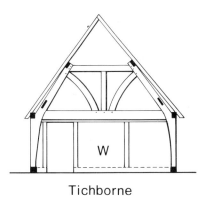

W

Tichborne

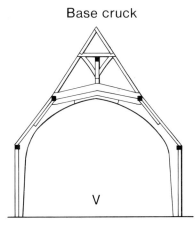

V

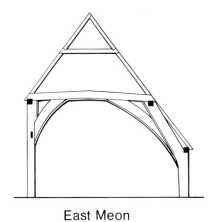

East Meon

Fig. 2 Diagram to show different types of apexes used to join cruck blades. Based on Alcock's classification with regional variations that appear in Hampshire.

15

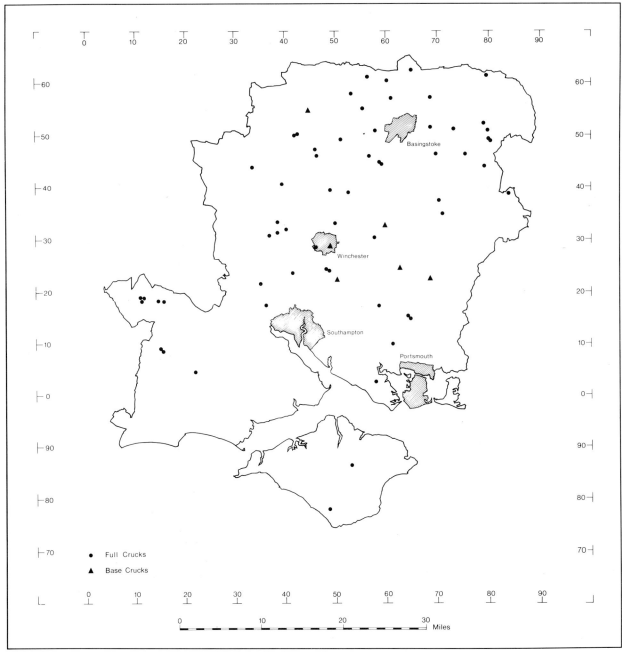

Fig. 3 Distribution of base crucks and full crucks in Hampshire

examples at Marwell (56), Riversdown (70) and the Pilgrims' Hall, Winchester (74). The Pilgrims' Hall has been dated by dendrochronology to about 1290 (Fletcher and Crook 1984, 130-133). But the surviving fragment of the hall at Mill Hill, Alresford (3), and the one-sided base cruck at Riverside suggest that this may be an accident of survival and that in fact smaller buildings were constructed using the technique even where it was hardly necessary as a means of roofing a very wide hall. It had in fact become a status symbol rather than a structural necessity. We may guess that its survival in smaller houses indicates a chronologically later use, perhaps appearing only in the mid fourteenth century.

Crucks

About the beginning of the fourteenth century a form of structure appeared in Hampshire with trusses formed of pairs of curved and inclined timbers today called crucks, also known to medieval craftsmen as 'forks'. These great curved blades were seated on sill beams or on stone foundations and bore the weight of the roof direct to the ground. In some cases, as at Twyford (5) the wall plates are supported on separate posts tied to the crucks by the tie beam halved round the crucks or by small spurs. In others, as at Tichborne (4), the plate and side purlin are carried on the outer face of the cruck, with windbraces either tenoned into the cruck or carried on the back. The crucks are joined at the top in a number of ways (Fig. 2). The classification used is that published in Alcock (1972). Most are designed to carry a ridge piece. In Hampshire the only roofs to have ridge pieces are cruck roofs, with the one exception of the king post and ridge roof of c.1300 at the Palace Stables at Bishop's Waltham (Mercer 1985, 95).

One type of cruck which has no ridge and with blades truncated at collar level is now classified as type W. Its distribution is widespread in those counties which border the edge of the cruck zone, notably Buckinghamshire. Many observers have been struck by the visual similarity between the base cruck and the truncated cruck, which has led in the past to some confusion in distinguishing between the two. Structurally they are distinct, the essential difference being that in a base cruck the longitudinal tie is the arcade plate, its soffit parallel to the ground, whereas a truncated cruck supports on the outside of the blade a side purlin which is angled to receive the rafters of the roof.

Despite the structural differences, chronologically it appears that some truncated crucks are contemporary with base crucks. Samples from cruck buildings in Berkshire submitted for radio carbon dating have produced a date of around 1275 and 1314 for two truncated crucks at Harwell and at Steventon (Currie and Fletcher 1972, 136). These, however, differ from the Hampshire examples in having archaic features such as two closely spaced collars and straight struts connecting arch braces to cruck blades, and it is also interesting that the arch braced truss in both cases is not the open hall truss but a closed truss. The Steventon example was rebuilt in the fifteenth century and we know from Hampshire examples that reuse of crucks in later building was not unknown, for example one of the closed cruck trusses at Tichborne (4) was formerly an open truss (possibly with two collars), while at No. 2 Forton, Longparish the tie beam from a cruck building was reused in a box framed hall. The small cruck hall from Boarhunt (32), now in the Wealden and Downland Museum, has a hall truss with truncated crucks, while the service end is post-built with a box frame and side purlin roof: if these features are contemporary, the house need not be earlier than the fifteenth century, but the possibility of the cruck truss being brought from elsewhere and reused should not be ruled out in the light of the early dating for the Berkshire truncated crucks. The form itself may be early, but the actual example can of course always be late. At Dogmersfield, Lords and Ladies (Mercer 1975, 163) has both a pair of truncated crucks and a pair with an F1 apex. For the present it is perhaps safest to assume that cruck buildings in Hampshire fall within the date range of 1330-1500 and that any apex types selected were a matter of convenience and local tradition rather than of chronological sequence.

Up to 1986, 58 cruck buildings had been found in Hampshire (Fig. 3). Of these four were barns, ten were houses with two-bay halls incorporating an arch-brace central truss and the remaining forty four were either one bay halls or fragmentary survivals where the number of bays could not be established. Of the apex forms (Fig. 2), type C was most common (nineteen examples) and type W had twelve examples. There were seven F1 types and four E types. H and V types were also represented sparsely. However, several houses had more than one apex type – seven had two types and three had three types. Type F1 with a short stud above the collar was generally present in these combinations suggesting it was used as a levelling device the stud of which could be cut down as required, where several pairs of crucks were of unequal height.

Alcock (1972, 61-81) noted that crucks appear rarely in towns but are often found in localised concentrations in villages such as Lacock, Coombe Bissett and Steeple Ashton in Wiltshire, or Lambourne and Compton in Berkshire. This pattern is matched in Hampshire where they occur in groups of two or more at Dummer, Twyford, Rockbourne and Kingsclere. But whereas in the Midlands, in Berkshire and Oxfordshire for example, cruck halls are sometimes found in combination with contemporary cross wings with crown post roofs, such a conjunction has not yet been recorded for Hampshire, except as a later development; at Pitt (59) for example a three-bay cruck house was extended by the addition of a box-framed cross wing with side purlin roof in the later fifteenth century. In Hampshire the typical cruck house plan is one of aligned bays, and this is also true of the small box framed house that gradually superseded it.

At what date cruck building was phased out altogether is difficult to establish. In Wales dendrochronology has shown that good cruck halls of the kind we see in Hampshire were being built as late as 1520-1560 (P.Smith pers. comm.). By this date in Hampshire box-framed houses have halls rising through two stories, the better to accommodate the floored bay at each end. The design of cruck building made this very difficult since floors were generally supported, as at Tichborne (4) at wall-plate level giving minimum headroom clearance on the first floor and corresponding difficulties with the stair, ventilation and light in what is no more than a loft. The use of jointed crucks to give extra height was the solution at The Crease (16) but apparently the idea was developed no further.

Box Framed Houses

Setting aside the constructional differences, the plan forms of the cruck-built houses, and those of the box frame houses are the same. Stoneacre, Denmead (22), and Garden Cottage, West Meon (21), are examples of the basic box-framed one-bay hall with service and parlour, while 78 Hursley (23) and Holbrook, Cheriton (20) represent the two-bay halls in this tradition. Of the cruck buildings in the district Embassy, Twyford (5) and Park View, Tichborne (4) are two-bay halls, and Ashley (6) and Park Cottage, Swanmore (68) have halls of one bay only. But all conform to the aligned bay plan. Most of the box framed halls have roofs with side purlins; the hall truss having arch braces, the collar either elaborately moulded as at Gable House, Bishop's Waltham (17), or perfunctory in the extreme as at Hursley (23).

This basic plan of aligned bays is subject to several variations in the internal arrangements of both constructional types. 78 Hursley illustrates the design at its simplest and most typical. There was a central hall with a parlour opening from it at the dais end. At the other end of the hall was a cross passage with two doorways leading to a service bay divided into two rooms.

At the higher end of the social scale, Littleton Manor (19) has the same plan form, although in a house of this size we might well expect a contemporary cross wing for the parlour. Holbrook, Cheriton (20) has a two-bay hall and a single floored bay, so it is possible a contemporary cross wing has been removed, and the same could be true of Gable House, Bishop's Waltham(17), which now has a later cross wing. But this is speculation, and it is an interesting characteristic of houses in central Hampshire that very few timber framed houses have contemporary cross wings. Exceptions are Gable House Bishops Waltham (17), Manor Farm, Botley (33) where only a fragment of the hall survives and Back Street, St Cross (60) which has a fine two storied parlour cross wing. It was normal for halls to be built of smaller size as time went on, and the single-bay hall can be a later feature besides a measure of economy in an early house. Garden Cottage, West Meon (21), is an example of a mid-fifteenth century house with a small single-bay hall, although attention to detail has not been neglected, with an internal jetty at the dais end and good plain carpentry. In date it is probably earlier than Littleton Manor (19) whose hall though of two bays with a fine arch brace truss, is yet only slightly longer than the adjacent floored bays. Monks Rest, Littleton (24), on design features probably contemporary with Littleton Manor (19), has the smallest hall of all. Our suggestion is that this was the house of the parish priest whose priority requirement was for a comfortable study.

"Wealden" and galleried houses

Wealden houses, so common in South-east England, are comparatively rare in Hampshire and of unconventional design. The form has many variations in Sussex and Kent, but the essential feature is that the chambers over the parlour and the service are jettied out over the ground floor wall on the front and sometimes ends or rear of the building. The other frequently associated feature is the crown post roof – a great rarity in Hampshire domestic architecture. Of the nine known examples of Wealdens in Hampshire, four lie in the Winchester area and all but one of them are in the eastern half of the county. Seven have side purlin roofs, the one exception being Boots the Chemist in Winchester High Street (11). There are two Wealdens in Wickham and one in Hambledon and these three (7-9) are

illustrated here since their differences from South-eastern Wealdens are instructive. Except for Boots they have side purlins and trussed rafter roofs, and single bay halls. They have slight means of support for the front plate of the hall since this was hardly necessary in a narrow, one-bay hall. Hampshire Wealdens are comparatively small and probably late, and the impression lingers of the local craftsmen following fashionable conventions for appearances' sake, while retaining their own well-tried constructional techniques.

It has been suggested that the continuous jettied house, floored throughout from the start, was a natural and immediate development from the Wealden house. In mid-Hampshire we have an intermediate form, the continuous jettied hall house. At the Curio Shop, Wickham (14), the jetty is balanced by an internal gallery giving access across the hall to the floored bays at either end of the house. At the Blue Boar, Winchester (13), there is a similar gallery which seems never to have been used for access. In Winchester (75), a range of 3-bayed units with a gallery across each hall was built by the Cathedral c.1460-71 on the site known as Godbegot (Keene 1985, 490-491). An unusual variant form is represented by The Crease, Micheldever (16), which has an extraordinary design featuring a box frame, continuous front jetty, a two-bay open hall and a jointed cruck to the hall truss, the front blade of which sits on the jetty. It is a building which, in its several parts, seems to exhibit all Hampshire's peculiarities.

Galleries to provide access across the hall are not confined to continuous jettied hall houses. Galleried halls have been identified in other parts of the country (Swain 1968, 127) but generally the gallery is an inserted feature as part of a post-medieval process of flooring the hall and confining the fire to a smoke bay. In Winchester, this process occurred at 36 Middle Brook Street (73), where the hall area, already curtailed by a side passage and gallery above, was further reduced by the addition of another gallery at right angles to the first (Keene 1985 158, 736-8). Nos. 33 & 34 High Street, Winchester (12) both set gable-end to the street, were probably a pair built together, each with a gallery with passage beneath to give access at first floor level across the hall, and this pattern seems to have been common in Southampton where inventories show that galleries were a notable feature of town houses there by the sixteenth century (Roberts forthcoming). Perry's Acre, Micheldever (15) is a rural example, a late medieval house in which the galleried hall has assumed the proportions of a smoke bay.

A popular device in central Hampshire was the internal jetty, where a floored bay, usually at the parlour end, projects into the hall, sometimes called an 'overshot' hall. This feature appears at the Blue Boar (13), Park View Tichborne (4) and at Garden Cottage, West Meon (21). The effect is to create a canopy over the high end of the hall; no doubt in imitation of the ornate canopies then to be found in the halls of the nobility.

In some cases the encroachment of the hall into the floored bay is taken even further, and the partition separating the hall from the parlour is absent at the time of construction, creating what is known as a half-floored hall. At Alexandra House, Wickham (8) the hall is so small that the inclusion of the whole of the floored space below the chamber makes a convenient canopy, given emphasis by the moulded dais beam. Here, as at Perry's Acre, Micheldever (15), and at Preshaw Farm Cottages (25), a separate parlour has been dispensed with, in favour of greater floor area to the hall which now occupies two bays on the ground floor and one bay of the first floor.

The typical Hampshire house is then a three- or four-bay building under one ridge, with three rooms, or sometimes two, on the ground floor. A variation on this has four rooms on the ground floor, including an extra room beyond the service, for example at Drove Cottage Compton (35), Church Lane, Martyr Worthy (26) and Preshaw Farm Cottages (25). The purpose and function of this extra room is rather puzzling. All three houses are substantial farmhouses with obviously well-to-do owners. An extra room beyond the service could be a dairy, or wellhouse; or extra storage space. In the case of Preshaw where there is some sign of blackening in the rafters above and evidence for the floor is missing. A suggested use is a kitchen or brewhouse integral to the house rather than a separate structure in the garden which is thought to have been the usual cooking arrangement of the medieval house.

81/82 Hursley (28) is another four-bay building with a specialised function. Floored throughout, with one long room on the ground floor, one room of three bays and another of one bay on the first floor, we suggest its use as a courthouse, where manorial business was carried out on the first floor which was accessible by an exterior staircase.

Roof types and dating evidence

The following types of roof construction have been identified in Hampshire:

1. Sans purlin, that is made up of pairs of common rafters each linked with a collar; example: Forge Sound (1) c.1350 associated with aisled or quasi aisled halls.

2. Ridge piece, king post roof: one example only, at Bishop's Waltham, Stables, c.1300 (Mercer 1985, 94-99).

3. Collar purlin roof, usually with a crown post: examples, Blue Boar, Winchester (13); Moysents, Bishop's Waltham (10), c. 1350. The crown post is usually short, square

sectioned and undecorated with the minimum of braces.

4a. Cruck with ridge piece. The crucks are joined at the top by a variety of apex types but dominated by type C: example, Little Thatches, Ashley (6) c.1450. The purlins are carried on the backs of crucks. Hall truss has arch brace.

4b. Cruck without ridge piece with truncated crucks, purlins carried on the backs of crucks. Hall truss has arch brace: example, Park View, Tichborne (4) c.1450.

5. Side purlin roof with principal rafters on a box frame. This type can have undiminished principals and threaded purlins as at Manor Farm, Botley (33), or diminished principals clasping purlins, always with a collar: example, Garden Cottage, West Meon (21). Closed trusses have a straight or cambered tie beam with three vertical struts to the collar: example, Littleton Manor (19) or with curved queen struts: example, Curio Shop, Wickham (14) or with raking struts to the principal rafters: example 3/4 High Street, Hambledon (9). The open hall truss has a cambered tie beam and arch braces often with a decorative moulding as at Gable House, Bishop's Waltham (17) c.1400. This type became the dominant one in Hampshire and lasted well into the seventeenth century.

The sans purlin roof (type 1) dates from as early as the thirteenth century and with its relative the collar purlin roof (type 3) continued in use into the fourteenth century (Smith 1958, 111-148). In Hampshire the continued use of the older types and the early employment of a comparative novelty, the side purlin roof, seem to have gone on side by side. It has been suggested that, in 1386, William of Wykham's carpenters were constructing the roofs over both the kitchen and the Long Room roof of New College, Oxford. (Hayter 1970, 42-46). The former has a side purlin roof with arch braces and two banks of wind braces, while the latter has a collar purlin roof supported by crown posts braced along the ridge only, a type we see again in Bishops Waltham Palace lodgings built by John Lewys in 1439 (Hare forthcoming). The hall and kitchen of St Cross Hospital, Winchester show a combination of side purlin roof in the hall, with crown post over the kitchen (if indeed they are contemporary) but the date of construction has been placed variously at 1372 (Hewett 1980, 287), after 1383 (Wood 1965, 29) and c. 1445 (Pevsner et al 1967, 712). East Meon courthouse of c.1425 has crown posts to both hall and chamber block (Wood 1965, 313). Bayleaf, a Kentish Wealden house with a crown post roof now in the

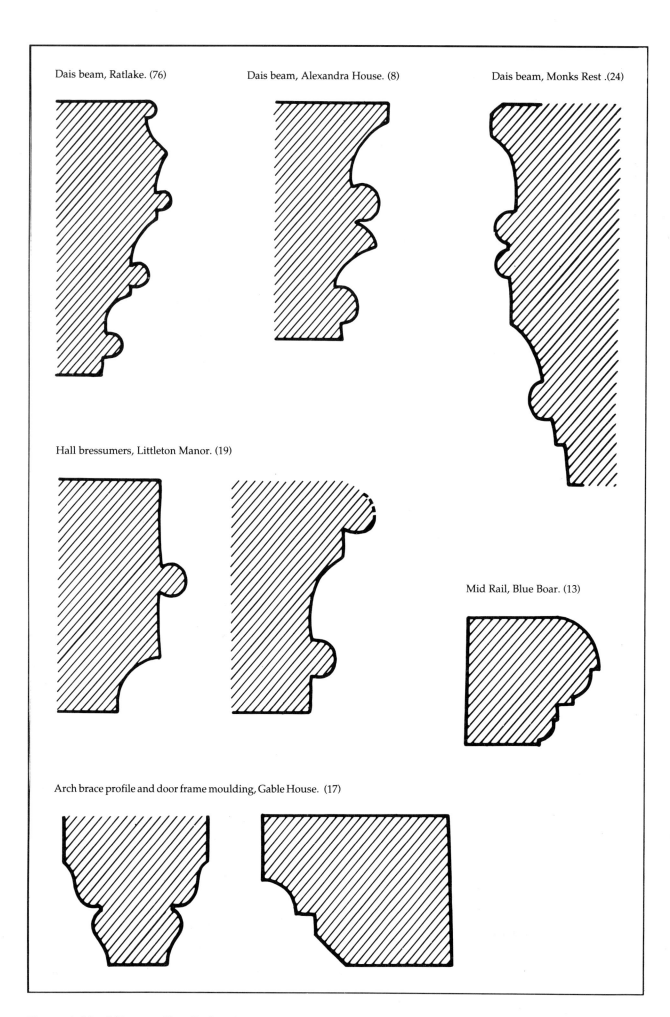

Dais beam, Ratlake. (76)

Dais beam, Alexandra House. (8)

Dais beam, Monks Rest .(24)

Hall bressumers, Littleton Manor. (19)

Mid Rail, Blue Boar. (13)

Arch brace profile and door frame moulding, Gable House. (17)

Figure 4. Moulding profiles. Scale 1:3

Wealden and Downland Museum has been dated to after 1405 by dendrochronology (Fletcher *et al* 1981, 38-39).

The unusual hybrid roof at Boots the Chemist which combines a crown post with side purlins suggests that Hampshire carpenters felt at ease with either type, but the side purlin roof was certainly the most favoured. Whereas in Surrey 110 crown post roofs of before 1600 have been counted to 118 clasped purlin roofs, of the same period (Harding 1980, 39-42), in Hampshire, (for which no comparable survey has been made) there is a mere handful of crown post roofs and the side purlin roof predominates. Our gazetteer for central Hampshire hall houses (page 00) lists 2 crown post roofs to 30 side purlin roofs and 6 crucks.

Internal fittings, wall framing and details

The flexibility and longevity of timber framing has enabled sound medieval buildings to be constantly upgraded to the present day, and perhaps the parts most vulnerable to change are the details, particularly the external framing which has often been taken out or the members cut through for new casement, sashed or bow windows. Consequently the only clues to the position of medieval windows may be a row of triangular or diamond-shaped holes in the soffit of the wall plate, indicating a row of mullions, or the survival of shutter grooves. The exterior wall framing may be concealed by mathematical or peg tiles, or faced with eighteenth century brick. Thatched roofs on rural buildings, and wooden shingles and Cornish slate on urban ones have been replaced by tile. Peg holes in the hall rafters are all that remain of timber louvres which controlled the issue of smoke from the open hearth at The Crease Micheldever (16) and Park View, Tichborne (4).

Another problem is establishing the position of the stairs, which in all cases have been moved, usually in consequence of the reorganisation that took place in the early seventeenth century when a chimney stack was inserted into the hall and an upper floor put in at the same time. Originally there would as a rule be two sets of stairs, one in the parlour and one in the service, and the interrupted medieval joists with a trimmer, for example at Gable House (17) or at Park Cottage, Swanmore (68), indicate the position. On occasion no such gap appears and one might postulate a ladder-like stair going directly up from the hall, for example at Park View, Tichborne (4) where there is a doorway in the wall between the hall and the chamber over the parlour. There are two examples at the Crease, Micheldever (16) and the Barracks, Wickham (7) where the access to the stair was through a door from the cross passage.

The form of these missing stairs may well have been solid oak blocks of triangular section such as those which survive at St Cross Hospital (Lloyd 1931, 451) at Rookwood Denmead (37) and in a sixteenth century house at Wickham called Budden's Farm.

The screen seems to be the most ephemeral of all features of the medieval house in this part of Hampshire, which raises the question of whether in some cases it was ever there at all – or whether a moveable screen, a piece of furniture or even a curtain was used instead. The base cruck halls at Riverside and Alresford apparently had no spere trusses, common in other parts of the country. Frequently screens are no more than projecting speres on each side of the hall acting as draught excluders to the opposed doorways and these may be decorated with chamfers or mouldings as at the Blue Boar (13) and the Crease (16). At Riverside (2), one of the earliest houses discussed, the speres are curved braces or brackets. At Park View, Tichborne (4) two opposing voided mortices in the wall plates at the end of the hall may have supported a bressumer for a screen.

Where it has been possible to reconstruct the wall framing, this is shown on the drawings, and it is clear from them what the main types were. In the earliest buildings at East Meon (1, 2), very long eccentrically curved braces are pegged into the bottom of the posts and reach the tie or wall plate, creating very large panels originally filled with wattle and daub.

The exterior framing is often the expression of the construction within, for example at Garden Cottage (21) where the side girt on the elevation marks the division between ground floor and first floor; it is not structually required in the hall bay so is there absent. At Park View Cottage, Tichborne (4), the flooring is supported at the plate level, creating a loft space and there is no side girt. Here only the end wall (now concealed) would have given any indication of its cruck construction, whereas on the elevations the crucks cannot be distinguished from the intermediate studs. As in most other cruck houses there are no braces on the side walls.

The Wealden form gives to the front elevation a strong distinction between floored and unfloored bays, particularly evident in the Barracks, Wickham (7). By the early sixteenth century bracing is zoned to the upper or the lower floor, even on the rear wall, and a typical pattern emerges of pairs of curved braces in each bay with a central stud. This pattern can be seen at Preshaw Farm Cottages (25) and at 81/82 Hursley (28). It is most impressive where there are many bays, as at Webbs Land Farm Barn, Wickham (29).

Tension bracing may be chronologically early since it appears on the Blue Boar and the front of the Chesil Rectory; and the St. Andrew's cross form appears on the facade of the Spinning Wheel café, all in Winchester and probably dating to the late fourteenth century. In general, arch bracing is more common than tension bracing. It appears on most of the fifteenth-century rural houses illustrated here, and a good example is the Priory Stables in Winchester Cathedral Close. The side walls of Littleton Manor (19), though now concealed, were of large panels with arch bracing, but the surviving end wall frame was of close studding, which began to come into fashion in the sixteenth century in this area.

Towards the mid 16th century timber scantlings became smaller and the framing of the walls was sub-divided into smaller, more regular panels with mid rails and short intermediate studs. Examples are Church Lane, Martyr Worthy (26) and Stapleford Farm, Durley (27). Mid rails and studs were also inserted about this time into earlier large-framed walls, providing reinforcement for large areas of wattle and daub. At Forge Sound (1) for example a number of inserted pieces have been introduced. These can usually be identified by the absence of peg holes suggesting non-morticed studs pushed in at random.

In other counties, particularly those in the west midlands and the south-east, carved designs are often found on salient features such as the spandrels of doorheads. By contrast, Hampshire gives the impression of plain, indeed austere, unornamented carpentry, with a lack of carving detail both on interior and exterior timbers. There are occasionally mouldings (never very elaborate or distinctive) on the hall bressumer, for example at Ratlake Ampfield (76), Alexandra House, Wickham (8) or Littleton Manor (19) (fig.5). Cusping occurs on decorative windbraces in Hambledon Manor (43) and on the hall truss at Tudor House, East Meon (18). In the main, the hall truss with arch braces and side purlins does not lend itself as a field for display. We would expect resources and demand for decorations to be evident in greater houses, such as those of the early sixteenth century in Northamptonshire which all exhibit carving, tracery and cusping on various roof elements (Meirion-Jones *et al* 1987, 34-40). In our area the hall of the Prior's house in Winchester is exceptional in having carved corbel heads, and pierced and chamfered quatre foil detail on the arch braces (Crook 1987a, 125-173).

Window heads are universally plain, with the exception of the decorated cusped ogee window head at the Blue Boar, with the close parallel at the Spinning Wheel Café, Winchester. The two shops in Winchester High Street (12) boast decorative cusped barge boards, which were once a feature of both Winchester and Salisbury houses. (RCHME 1980).

Non-domestic buildings

The techniques of timber framing in aligned bays that enabled carpenters to produce small hall houses were appropriate to other buildings, many much larger and of multiple bays. Surviving farm buildings were of manorial status – Webbs Land Farm barn (29) of ten bays and the seven bay building we interpret as a sheep house (30). Although very well-built cruck barns survive in north Hampshire, so far none have been found in this area. In their time these buildings were as economically important as banks are today and the key to the wealth of large estates, and corresponding care and expense was lavished on their construction and appearance. Similarly, buildings put up for the use of the community (and equally of benefit to the landlord) are also well made and carefully planned, such as 81-82 Hursley (28) which was probably designed as a courthouse. The barns and outhouses which were attached to many peasant farms have not been indentified for this period.

Summary and Conclusions

The smaller hall houses of central Hampshire built between c. 1350 and 1550 are undistinguished by their decorative quality and perhaps that is why they have been in general unnoticed by the passing antiquary. Many have been rebuilt or replaced in the seventeenth or eighteenth centuries and the external appearance of villages in mid Hampshire is of a picturesque but predominantly post-medieval stock of houses of a very simple kind. There is little comparison here with the Surrey villages like Charlwood with its clusters of medieval houses round the Common (Harding 1976) or Nuffield and Burstow (Gray 1980, 10) with some 18 hall houses in two parishes; closer appraisals of individual parishes are however needed for Hampshire.

Representatives of almost every category of medieval building survive here, albeit on a modest scale and with local variations. The area is particularly strong in aisled and quasi-aisled halls of which only the smaller examples are illustrated here. In recent years discoveries of cruck-built houses have filled in the distribution map for Hampshire (Fig. 3) without extending its eastern limit which remains a remarkably distinct frontier. The number surviving and the consistency of the basic designs argues that the cruck type was well established and supremely successful as a smaller house type. It is much rarer to find a good example of a box-frame house with a roof type demonstrably earlier than the side purlin (that is before 1450). Hampshire carpenters looked both westwards and eastwards for building ideas, adopting both crucks and Wealdens, but bringing to them certain details and modifications of their own. The rural hall house with an integral gallery seems to be a type almost unique to Hampshire[1], while The Crease (16) stands alone as a unique combination of different ideas and constructional techniques, concentrated in one building.

[1] Habberley Hall in Shropshire has galleries on all four sides of a central smoke bay (E. Mercer pers.comm.).

Part Two

**Small Houses
in mid Hampshire, c.1550**

The documentary evidence

Probate inventories and their interpretation

This book describes and illustrates over twenty surviving medieval houses in mid-Hampshire. In most cases the physical or archaeological evidence is sufficiently complete for us to be reasonably confident as to the number of rooms in each house; from three rooms at Embassy Cottage, Twyford (5) to seven rooms at the cottages off Church Lane, Martyr Worthy (26).

The physical evidence tells us much of interest, but we would like to know more about the people who lived in these houses. What kind of people were they, what life style did they enjoy and how did they use the various rooms in their houses? To answer these questions we must turn to the documentary evidence. This is severely limited for the 14th and 15th centuries. However, for the 16th century we have the probate inventories which, in Hampshire, survived in quantity after 1545. The most useful inventories list, in detail, the contents of each room in the house of the deceased. A hundred of these inventories have been selected for analysis dating from between 1545 and 1558, and covering the same geographical area as the houses described in this book[1]. Thus the archaeological and documentary evidence can be compared. Assuming that the number of rooms per house is a rough indicator of the social status of the occupants, these inventories can tell us about the social status that a house had achieved by 1550. However, the appraisers who drew up the inventories did not always clearly distinguish between integral rooms and out-buildings. Thus the calculation of the number of rooms per house is, to an extent, a matter of judgement[2].

Of the 262 inventories from our geographical area which date from between 1545 and 1558, 162 make no reference – or possibly an incomplete reference – to rooms. We cannot know how many rooms these houses had, but a significant number may have been one-roomed houses since such houses are presumed to have been common. "The absence of any listing of rooms in some of the smallest inventories..... may well indicate that there was only one room and therefore no need to distinguish where the household goods lay" (Hoskins, 1963,105). If this is so, it may explain why there are only two houses, or hovels of one room recorded in our sample. In one of them lived John Sutar of Micheldever whose sole room was called 'the hall'. Into this room he contrived to squeeze various pots and pans, pothangers and platters, a flitch of bacon hanging in the roof, two spinning wheels, seven tubs, a bill, a saddle, a board for a trestle table, a few clothes, an old featherbed and "other broken gear". Out of doors, John Sutar had a mere two acres of wheat, one acre of vetches, a cow, a horse and ten sheep (HRO U. wills 1553/200).

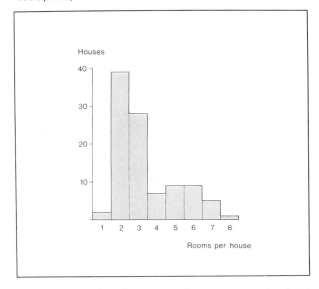

Fig. 5 The number of rooms per house in a sample of 100 probate inventories from mid Hampshire, 1545-1558

1. In the Hampshire Record Office there are 262 inventories dating from between 1545 and 1558, and which derive from 45 rural parishes and 4 small towns in our area. Slightly over 100 of the inventories mentioned rooms, but a few of these were judged to be incomplete or unsatisfactory for our purposes, leaving a sample of exactly 100. No suitable inventories appear to be at the Public Record Office (Smith 1984, 1-2). Apart from inventories, there are other promising 16th century sources which were, unfortunately, too diverse and scattered to be systematically used.

2. The general problems associated with use of inventories have been fully discussed elsewhere (Priestley et al 1982, 94-97; Moore 1985, 11-18), but a few points need to be emphasised here. Firstly there is the need to compare like with like. Since our focus is on the smaller medieval house, the inventories of larger houses with 9 rooms or more have been excluded from consideration. Secondly, since most of the surviving houses described are in a rural setting, the inventories relating to town houses in central Winchester have been excluded, but it was not clear how inventories from small towns should be treated. On balance, it was decided to include them, since surviving medieval houses in the small towns of New Alresford (3), Wickham (7, 8 and 14) and Hambledon (9) were built with the ridge parallel to the street frontage and were, in general, structurally similar to rural houses; whereas houses in central Winchester (12, 73 and 75) were frequently built end-on to the street, with a consequent difference in structure and form. Thirdly, the size of the sample is unavoidably small. It is limited by the need to select inventories which derived from the same geographical area as the surviving houses, and by the undesirability of straying too far after 1550, the end of our period. It was especially necessary to select only those inventories which appeared to list every room in a house, although we could not be sure whether rooms had been deliberately omitted (Moore 1985, 15), and the appraisers did not always distinguish between integral rooms and out-buildings. Lastly, it has been assumed that the number of rooms per house is a rough indicator of the social status of the occupants only at the time when the inventories were taken in 1545-58. However, it is probable that the inventories record houses of variable age; some were then brand new and others perhaps 200 years old. Thus a 3-roomed house of c.1350, for example Forge Sound, East Meon (1), was probably built for a man of substance. By 1550 it may have slipped down the social scale as wealthier peasants copied the fashion for more rooms and greater privacy (Hoskins 1963, 144).

Thirty-nine of the inventories in the sample record two-roomed houses and it has plausibly been suggested that these consisted essentially of a single room, crudely partitioned to create a relatively private and smokeless sleeping chamber (Hoskins 1963,105), Richard Morrall of Brown Candover lived in such a two-roomed house. His hall contained the necessary gear for cooking and eating, together with sundry tools, while "a chamber at the end of the hall" was reserved for his bed (HRO U. wills 1557/448). Thus 41, or over two fifths, of the houses recorded by the inventories in the sample had one or two rooms. That is, they had fewer rooms than any medieval house so far discovered in central Hampshire. Such houses were either too flimsy or too small to be preserved and they have long been replaced by better-built and roomier dwellings.

The appraisers rarely bothered to mention the trade or social rank of the deceased, probably because the great majority were husbandmen, or humble peasant farmers and farmworkers. However, in 10 inventories from the sample, the deceased is specifically called a 'husbandman'. All these husbandmen occupied two or three-bedroomed houses, whereas the five men called 'yeoman' occupied houses of between three and seven rooms. Thus, on this evidence, only Forge Sound (1) and Embassy Cottage (5), of the houses described in this book, would have ranked in 1550 as dwellings suitable for a husbandman although they could also be described as houses for poor yeoman. Others, from Riverside, East Meon (2), with four rooms to the cottages at Martyr Worthy (26) with seven rooms, would have been typical yeomen's houses. It would, however, be unwise to make too precise a distinction between yeoman and husbandmen on the basis of a relatively small sample (Harries 1986, 11).

Turning to a specific example, Robert Applegarth of Ropley was a wealthy yeoman whose house had seven rooms. In his hall was a table, with two forms and three chairs, where he and his family sat to eat. The walls were hung with three painted or stained cloths. Andirons and pothangers indicate a fire which burnt in a chimney or smoke bay, for the hall had been floored to create a chamber over the hall. Such rooms were often created for storage and for second bedrooms (Barley 1967,737) and here sacks of malt and hops lay alongside three beds, probably for children. The best bed chamber was generally downstairs next to the hall (Barley 1961,43) and it is likely that Robert Applegarth himself slept here. In this chamber were his apparel, including his gown and three coats, two featherbeds, and some fine napery. In the buttery were, amongst other items, drinking glasses, silver spoons, salt, oatmeal and tallow. Also in the house were a servants' chamber with six beds, a maidens' chamber (possibly for the female servants) and a porch chamber with more beds. This large and prosperous household was supplied with food from its own kitchen, malthouse and barn (HRO U. wills 1553/4).

The six inventories from the sample which specifically refer to craftsmen's houses, record dwellings which range from two to seven rooms. At the lower end of the social scale was Robert Cardy, a blacksmith of East Tisted, who lived in a humble dwelling with only a chamber and hall; his kitchen and his blacksmith's shop were probably separate from the house[3] (HRO U.wills 1557/126). At the other end of the scale was Eusby Croppe, a weaver of New Alresford, who lived in a seven-roomed house comprising a chamber, a hall, a shop within the hall, a great shop with looms, a men's chamber for servants or apprentices, a wool loft and a cellar. His kitchen and warehouses were probably detached from the main dwelling (HRO B.wills 1551/48).

The five clergymen's houses in the sample had from three to seven rooms each. Thomas Watson, the parson of King's Worthy, lived in a seven-roomed house, to which belonged a brewhouse, a bakehouse and a kitchen which were probably detached (HRO B.wills 1556/205). On a more modest scale, William Hatton the parson of Ovington had only a hall, chamber and buttery in his house, with a kitchen which again was probably detached (HRO U.wills 1550/76). Although this was a small house, it may have been built with a quality and pretension similar to Monks' Rest (24), another small parsonage which survives at Littleton. As for the gentry, only one gentleman's house was sufficiently small to fall within the sample. Henry Goldsmith, a gentleman of Exton, lived in a six-roomed house (HRO B.wills 1554/109). Probably more typical of this class, however, was Tichborne House, where Nicholas Tichborne esquire had fifteen rooms and numerous outhouses. (HRO B.wills 1555/78).

In 1550, the hall was still the principal room in small houses in mid-Hampshire, as it probably had been throughout the Middle Ages. All the one hundred houses in the sample had halls and 89 inventories list the hall first, reflecting both its importance and the need for the appraisers to enter a house through the hall doorway, or through the screens passage at the end of the hall. All the halls in the sample had tables and seats for family meals and a great majority of halls were open to the rafters, since they had no chambers above. In ten of the larger houses there was a chimney or smoke bay in the hall, which allowed the insertion of a floor. Strangely, only half the halls in the sample (51 out of 100) had andirons, pothangers, or other evidence of fire, although the absence of fire was much commoner amongst inventories taken in the summer. It may be that in some households, by 1550, the hall fire was reserved for heating during the winter months, whilst cooking had been relegated to the kitchen. If so, this is a rather

---

3. The problem of deciding whether kitchens and service rooms were integral to the main house, attached as lean-to structures, or entirely detached, is touched on in note 2 (above) and discussed with reference to kitchens (below). Ultimately, the inventories do not allow us to solve the problem with certainty.

early example of the transposition of cooking from hall to kitchen in humble households (Barley 1967, 737.)

Most houses in the sample (82 out of 100) had kitchens. Although some kitchens were used simply for storing food, the majority (70 out of 100) of kitchens had fires for cooking meals. This might suggest that most houses had two integral rooms with hearths. However, this fails to match the physical evidence for, of the houses which we have examined, only Preshaw Farm Cottages (25) may have had both an open hall and another integral room which may have been a kitchen. The weight of the physical evidence supports the view that most of the kitchens referred to in the inventories were similar to the small detached outhouses noted in this period in Sussex (Martin 1977-87, i 18). In a majority of cases (59 out of 82), the kitchen is listed just before, or among the outhouses and occasionally there is specific reference to "the kitchen and other houses" (HRO U wills 1557/613), although the word 'house' could sometimes refer to an integral room.

Sixteen of the inventories record butteries, which were generally in the larger dwellings. These butteries were used for storing crockery, pans and spoons on shelves and for keeping drink in vats or barrels. Some houses – for example the Crease, Micheldever (16) – had divided service bays. Although one service room may have been called 'the buttery', the inventories do not make clear what the other was called. Within the sample of 100 inventories, 8 brewhouses were recorded, 7 boulting-houses where bread was prepared, 3 dairy-houses, 2 well houses, 3 malthouses and 2 bakehouses. Although the term 'house' could apply to an integral room, these service rooms were often detached or distinct from the main house, an hypothesis supported by their placement towards the end of the inventories. Over one third of the inventories (36) record barns and about one sixth (14) record stables. These farm buildings were almost certainly much smaller than manorial farm buildings (e.g. 29 and 30) and none seems to have survived. Similarly no physical evidence for medieval kitchens and outhouses belonging to small dwellings has been found in mid-Hampshire.

The inventories suggest that in mid-sixteenth century Hampshire, no beast shared the same house with man, as they did in the long houses typical of some northern and western regions of Britain. However, the farm invaded the house in other ways; axes, scythes, shears and other farm implements were kept almost at random in any room, and wool, malt and barley were stored in the lofts. For although today the small timber-framed house in a Hampshire village is likely to be the dormitory home of a city worker, or until recently a farm labourer's cottage, in the sixteenth century it was almost invariably the centre for a small farm. Even men whose principal occupation was not farming, such as Thomas Watson, the parson of King's Worthy, and John Prat, a clothier from Hambledon, kept farms as sidelines. Although some craftsmen in market towns seem not to have farmed at all, it was not uncommon to find small-holdings in towns. At New Alresford, Nicholas Lyde the dyer kept poultry and had 2 acres of wheat while Euseby Croppe the weaver kept poultry, pigs and a cow (HRO B.wills 1551/48 and 120; 1556/114 and 205).

In conclusion, the picture that emerges from the documentary evidence is of a Spartan and cramped existence for the poorer peasant and husbandman. At this level, the hall was the only heated room in the house and generally the only room in which there was a rough bench on which to take one's ease. Even among the wealthier yeomen, craftsmen and parsons, the inventories record no window glass, a heated parlour was a rarity and only one reference has been found to a stair, in contrast to the ladder which was still the usual way to upper rooms in smaller houses (Portman 1964,162). Elsewhere in the house beds might be crammed as many as six to a room alongside tools which today would be relegated to a garden shed. However, among these wealthier folk small luxuries indicate that life had risen above a mere struggle for survival. Stained cloths to decorate the walls and silver spoons and pewter to impress the neighbours were common, while cheese in the loft, flitches of bacon and ample stores of corn show that this class could enjoy a well-fed, if simple existence.

Two inventories from the sample

John Sutar of Micheldever, 19th March 1553 (HRO U.wills. 1553/200)

Imprimis, 2 busshells of Rie, 14d; A quarter of barly, 6s.8d.; 3 busshells of mawlte, 2s.6d.; 2 acres of wheat in the feld, 6s.8d.; one acre of vaches, 20d.; a horse, 12d,; a cowe, 8s.; 10 sheppe, 13s.4d.; and an old carre, 8d.; one flycke of bacon in the rowffe, 2s.; 2 pygs, 2s.

IN THE HALL.   2 brasse pannes, 4s.; 2 potts and kettells, 3s.4d.; a frying panne, 2 candlesticks, a tryvet, a broche, a potte hanger, 2 saucers and other broken gear with a byll, 20d,; one plate, 3 potingers, 2 saucers and a salte seller, 16d.; 7 tubbs, 2s.4d.; a woullen wheele and a lynen wheele, 12d.; a red saddell, 8d.; 3 bords, 2s; a hatt and a night capp, 8d.; a gowne, 6s.8d.; a woosted jacket, 3 cottes, a dublet, 2 jerkens, 10s.; a payer of hosses, 2s.4d.; a old cloke, 12d.; 3 sherts, 20d.; 3 coffers, 6s.; a woodknyffe, 4d.; a old fetherbed and a matteris, 5s.; 3 payer of sheets, a coverlet, a blancket and a bolster with the haings (hangings?) and a pillowe, 3s.4d.; in redie money, £18.

SUM TOTAL: £22.19s.

Robert Aplegarth of Ropley (yeoman)
29th January 1553 (HRO U.wills 1553/4)

IN THE HAULE. One cupboard, 5s.; a table, two formes and three chayers, 5s.; thre stayned clothes, 2s.; a cupboard clothe and a towell, 3s.; two pothangers and two awndyerns, 3s.; sum 18s.

THE CHAMBER Two fetherbedds and a mettres, two bolsters, a payer of blanketts, a payer of sheets, a pyllowe, two coverletts and a tester over the bedd, 30s.; one flockebedd, a bolster, a coverlette, a payer of sheets and a tester over the bedd, 10s.; two bedsteeds, 16d.; a byll and a gleve, 20d.; 7 coffers and a presse, 16s.;
sum 59s.

Napery. 6 payer of canvas sheets and a fyne sheete, 30s.; a tester to hange over a bed of canvas, 2s.4d.; two table clothes of dyaper, 23s.4d.; three table clothes of canvas, 5s; two dyaper towells, 5s.; fower pyllow-beers, 3s; 9 table napkyns, 6 of dyaper and 3 of lokaram, 2s. sum £3.10.8d.

Apparell. A gowne, three coots, 3 doubletts and thre payer of hose, £5; two sherts, 5s; 6 yardes of newe clothe, 9s.; sum £5.14s.

THE BUTTERYE. 4 candelstycks, 2s.; 3 drynkynge glasses, 2s.; 10 silver spones, 20s; fower drynkynge cuppes and a tanked, 4d; 5 vyrkyns and foure tubbes, 4s.6d; 6 olde tubbes 16d; 4 busshells of white salte, 3s.4d; 4 earthen potts full of grece conteynynge three gallonds, 4s; 4 lether bottells, 16d; two busshells of oote meale, 2s.8d; three pounde of tallowe, 6d; sum 42s.

THE MAYDENS CHAMBER. A coverlet, two blanketts, a bolster and a payer of shets,10s.; a syde saddell, 2s., a sheffynge seve, 12d.; 8 riphooks, 12d.; a pece of clowtinge lether, 12d.; an iron bealme and a payer of skales, 12d; sum 16s.

THE PORCHE CHAMBER. A fetherbed, a flockbed, a payer of sheets, a coverlett, two bolsters, a pyllowe and a pyllowbere, 26s.8d.; a bedstead, 8d.; a carpett for a borde, 2s.; sum 29s.4d.

THE CHAMBER OVER THE HAWLE. two fether-beds, a coverlett, a bolster and a payer of sheets, 26s.8d.; a bedstead, 8d.; a flockbedd, fyve pyllowes, 3 blanketts and two bankers for benches, 20s.; a tester for a bedd, 2s.; half a hundreth of hoppes, 8s.; 4 quarters of malte, 40s.; sum £4.17s.4d.

THE SERVANTS CHAMBER. A flockbedd, a bol-ster, a coverlett and a payer of sheets, 10s.; a mattris, a coverlett, a blankett and a payer of sheets, 6s.8d.; an other bedd with the'apparell, 3s.4d.; 4 bedsteades, 2s.; 4 qwyssyons, 12d; two olde saddells, 4s.; a bry-dell, 12d.; a payer of boots and a payer of sporis, 2s; a seadlyppe, 4d.; sum 30s.4d.

THE KYCHYN. 4 brasse potts, three brasse pannes, 4 kettells, a cawthern and one possenett, 53s.4d.; a furneys, 10s.; 4 spytts, a payer of lyttell covyerns, two trevetts, two fryenge pannes, an oven peale, two gredyerns and two payer of pott hooks, 10s.; a lyttell brasse pott, a skymmer, a chafying dysshe and a payer of bellowes, 3s.; one charger, a basen and an ewer, 18 platters, 14 pottyngers, 21 saucers, 4 pewter dysshes, 4 salte sellers, two pewter cuppis, a great pewter potte, and olde flaggon of pewter, 43s.4d.; one platter and a pottynger of pewter and half a dosen of sponys, 18d.; a wymvynge sheete and a hearclothe 3s.4d.; a dosen of trenchers, 1d.; the brewynge vessells, viz. two vates, two kyvers, two barrells and two buckets, 7s.; two hedgynge bylls, two axes, 4 iron wedges and an iron barr, 5s.; a todd weight of lead, and half a todd, a three pounde and two pounde, 2s.; two mattocks, 3 shovells, a dunge pyke and two prongs, 3s.4d.; 3 awgers, a chesyll, a hansaw and a sarpe, 16d.; 11 hogges of baken and foure sydes of beef, 53s.4d.; sum £9.16s.7d.

THE MALTHOUSE. Two vates, two trowes, a chese presse, a round table and a cowle, a well bucket and a rope, 13s.4d.; three malt seves, three wymvynge seves and three rydders, 16d.; sum 14s. 8d.

THE CORNE IN THE BARNE. Peas and vetches, £3.13s.4d.; 24 quarters of wheat, £12; 30 quarters Barley £15; 13 quarters otes, £4.6s.8d; sum £35.

THE CORNE IN THE FIELD. 29 acres of wheat, £7.5s.; 6 acres of vetches, 20s.; sum £8.5s.

THE CATTELL. Six horses and their harnes with two carts, a ploughe and harrowes with th'appertenan-cys, £13.6s.8d.; 7 kyne and a bull, £5.6s.8d.; two oxen, 46s.8d.; Three bullocks of two yeres of age and three other of one yere of age, 40s.; 9 score wethers £19; 60 ewes and rammes £6; 50 teggs, £3.6s.8d.; 21 hogges, 40s. A bore and two sowes, 10s.; sum £53.16s.8d.

THE PULTRY. One cock and 6 hennes, 20d.; Two mallerds and ten ducks, 2s.; A gander and two gese, 18d.; sum 5s.2d.

SUM TOTAL: £131. 14. 9d.

Part Three

**Description of selected
medieval buildings**

29

1

Forge Sound, East Meon

Grid Ref: SU 682221

A single-aisled hall. c. 1350.

Forge Sound: east elevation. (PMJC)

This building is unusual both as a rare survival of an aisled hall and for its remarkable state of preservation for such an early house.

Forge Sound stands in a triangle of ground between the river Meon and the Hambledon road leading from East Meon village. The house is end on to the road and parallel to Riverside (2), a house of similar date. The space between these two houses is about 30 feet wide and may have originated as a medieval lane leading across the river to East Meon Court House (40).

The roof is now tiled and has a full hip at both ends. The original framing of the north and east elevations is in an unusually good state of preservation, considering the great age of the house. (The sill on the east side rests on a flint plinth.) Long passing braces run from the feet of principal posts up to the wall plates, thus creating large triangular panels (see exterior reconstruction). Three posts on the eastern wall indicate the probable positions of the hall window and of the original door at the southern end of the hall, where indeed the front door is today. This door opens into a cross passage whose inserted partition may echo an original screen.

It is a three-bay house. The two northern bays (A–C) comprise a well-preserved single-aisled hall. Both bays of the hall are approximately 9 feet in length. The nave of the hall is 14 feet wide and the aisle is 3 feet 9 inches wide.

In the cross frames at either end of the hall are the remains of great passing braces, which ran from the tie beams almost to the feet of the principal posts (cross section A/A'). An arch braced, cambered tie beam crosses the centre of the hall (cross section B/B') and arch braces spring from the arcade posts to the arcade plate (long section). This arcading has a close parallel in the early fourteenth century Stanton's Farm at Black Notley, Essex (Wood, 1965, 303).

The sans-purlin roof has a smoke gablet at the northern end of the hall. Each pair of common rafters is joined by a collar which is halved into the rafters with dovetail lap joints. The rafters in both the nave and aisle of the hall are heavily soot-blackened. This alone provides strong evidence that the aisle is an original feature and not an added outshot. In addition, the aisle rafters are neatly joined extensions of the nave rafters and the aisle tie at B is well morticed both to the arcade post and to the aisle wall plate. Lastly, the arcade post rests on a pad stone and there is no evidence that it ever rested on a sill beam, which would have been a necessary feature had it originally formed part of an outside wall.

The scarf joints in arcade and wall plates are side pegged and there are no dragon ties. The southern floored bay is approximately 13 feet long. The joists in this bay are at present concealed.

A floor has been inserted into the hall. Two small extensions have been built on the north and west side of the house, that on the north housing a chimney stack.

1

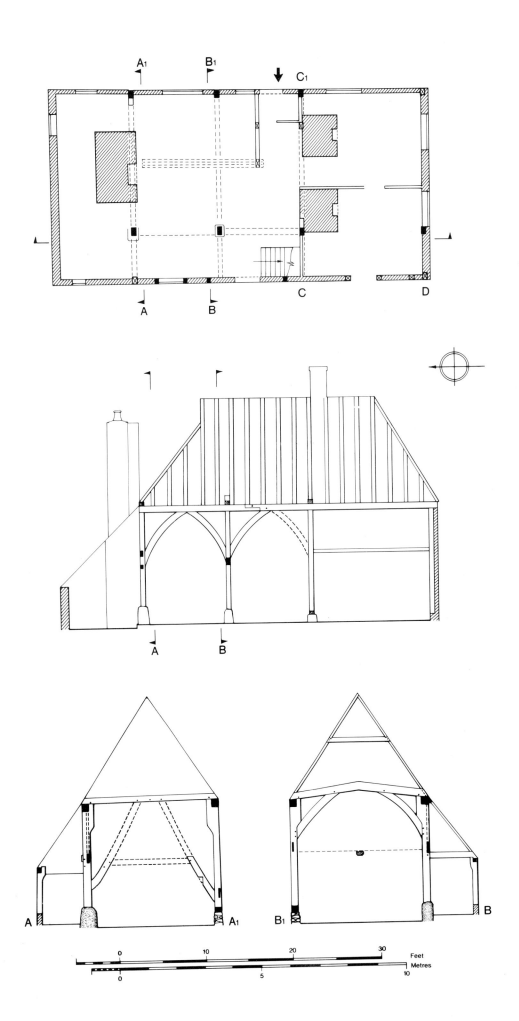

A₁   B₁   ↓ C₁

A   B   C   D

A   B

A   B

A   A₁   B₁   B

0   10   20   30   Feet
Metres
0   5   10

Forge Sound looking towards the north end of the hall.

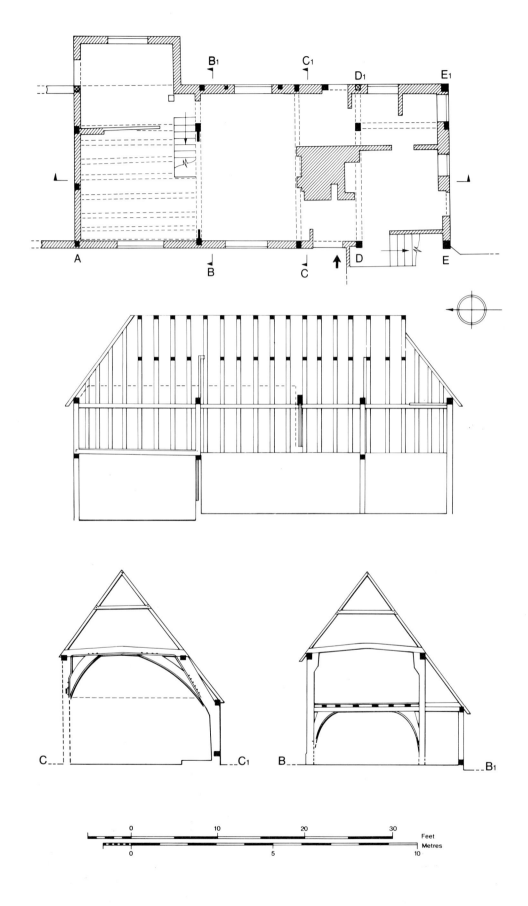

2

Riverside, East Meon

Grid Ref: 682221

A hall house with single aisle and base cruck c.1350

Riverside stands between the river Meon and the Hambledon road leading out of East Meon village. It is end on to the road and parallel to Forge Sound (1), a house of similar date. Like Forge Sound it is remarkable as an early house in a fine state of preservation.

Riverside is a four-bay house, with a full hip at both ends of the roof. The roof has neither purlins, nor principal rafters and each pair of common rafters is joined by a collar which is halved into the rafters with dovetail lap joints. The roof is heavily soot-blackened in the hall (B-D) and service bay (D-E). At this end of the house, below a smoke gablet are curved dragon ties which run horizontally between tie beam and wall plate, and tie beam and arcade plate respectively.

Riverside: south elevation showing the single aisle and fragmentary long braces. (JRB)

The nave of the house is 12 feet wide between posts, and the aisle is 3 feet 6 inches. The hall truss comprises a base cruck, which spans the aisle, and a cambered tie beam which is braced by arch braces springing from the base cruck on the east and a principal post on the west (section C/C'). The post, base cruck, tie beam and arch braces which form this truss are chamfered on both sides. The hall is of two unequal bays, the upper end (B-C) being 10 feet 6 inches in length while the lower end (C-D) measures

only 7 feet in length. At present the front door opens into what was the lower end of the hall and this is probably the original position of the house entrance. However, there is no sign of a cross passage and, indeed, there was hardly room for one in a bay measuring only 7 feet.

Bay A-B was floored to make a parlour with chamber above. The original flooring over the aisle has been destroyed. This area probably contained the original stair, since the joists in the nave of the parlour bay are substantially intact and bear no evidence of a trimmer. The parlour was open to the hall, but the entrance was partly screened with heavy, chamfered braces. This feature is paralleled in a closely comparable single quasi-aisled hall at Homewood House, Bolney Sussex (Mason 1957, 85-90) Above the bressummer this bay was closed (cross section B/B' and long section). The parlour bay is 13 feet long, the same length as the parlour bay at Forge Sound (1). The total length of the halls at Riverside and Forge Sound differs by no more than 6 inches. Indeed, many features of Riverside and Forge Sound echo each other and it is difficult not to conclude that they were designed by the same builder.

The hall was closed from a small service bay at the southern end of the house. Evidence for this closure lies in (i) mortices for studs in the bressummer soffit, (ii) wattle and daub between collar and tie beams. In this truss (D/D') are remnants of great passing braces, similar to those at Forge Sound. The service bay is not floored and appears never to have been so. The dragon ties would not admit floor joists and a first floor would have been of little use on account of the slope of the hipped roof and the limited length of the bay, a mere 8 feet 6 inches. In the southernmost wall of the house are braces which could be described as the lower halves of passing braces, again similar to those found at Forge Sound. In this wall there is an aisle tie and it is probably that each truss has or had an aisle tie, although the evidence for this is at present obscured.

A wattle and daub chimney was inserted in the lower bay of the hall (C-D). This was superseded by a brick chimney and the upper bay of the hall (B-C) was floored. A sixteenth century building on a different alignment has been added to the south-west corner of Riverside.

Riverside: interior of the hall looking north

3
Mill Hill, Alresford
Grid Ref: SU 587329

A base cruck hall of c.1350

Mill Hill, Alresford: the base cruck hall survives between two
later cross wings. (PMJC)

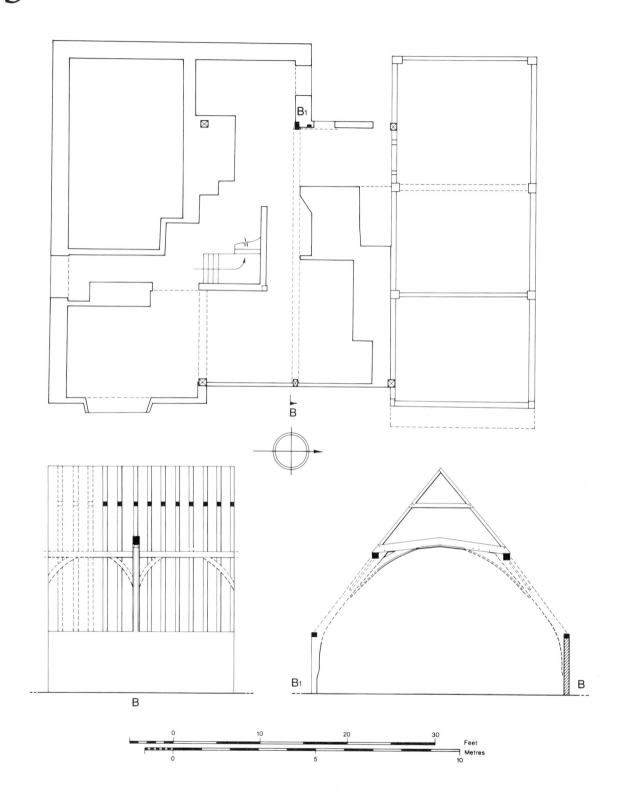

B₁

B

B

B₁

B

| 0 | 10 | 20 | 30 | Feet |
| 0 | | 5 | | 10 | Metres |

The house stands lengthwise to the street at the junction of Broad Street, the main market of the medieval town, and Mill Hill. It occupies a large burgage plot 66 feet wide (four perches) instead of the 33 feet wide plot more usual in Alresford. The exterior presents the appearance of an H-plan with two projecting cross wings, however both of these are later additions and replace the original end walls of the hall and may even truncate the hall itself.

Fragmentary remains of a two bay open hall survive and these suggest that it was originally about 22 feet long by 28 feet wide, although only part of the central hall truss (B/B') and neither of the end trusses survive. We do not know whether there was more than one truss to the hall, or how the service and parlour bays were laid out, whether in axial bays or in cross wings.

Of the original timbers, there remain the common rafters which are joined to the collars by dovetail lap joints, most of the two arcade plates and the tie. The base cruck and brace on the west side are present though partly concealed. The reconstruction offered is based on these elements and it will be seen we favour a full base cruck rather than the one aisled type seen at Riverside, East Meon. This case is supported by the mortices on the soffits of the arcade plates which are angled to allow for windbraces in the roof plane, whereas they would be in a vertical plane if they were intended to receive the studding for a front wall.

The form of the base cruck is simple and undecorated except for a chamfer along the collar continued onto the brace. The scantlings are small and comparable with those at East Meon (1, 2) rather than those of impressive scale found at Riversdown (70), Marwell (56), or the Pilgrims' Hall, Winchester (Crook 1982, 85-101). The Alresford example falls short of the social standing of these buildings although in scale and position it must have been of some local significance.

The timber-framed cross wing at the north end was added in the mid-sixteenth century, its east elevation jettied on to the street, while the brick and timber extension on the south was built along with the staircase in the seventeenth century when the hall was floored and the chimney inserted. The position of the east wall of the hall was retained and rebuilt in brick, after the removal of the base cruck on this side.

[The help of Dr N. Alcock in surveying and assessing this building is acknowledged.]

4

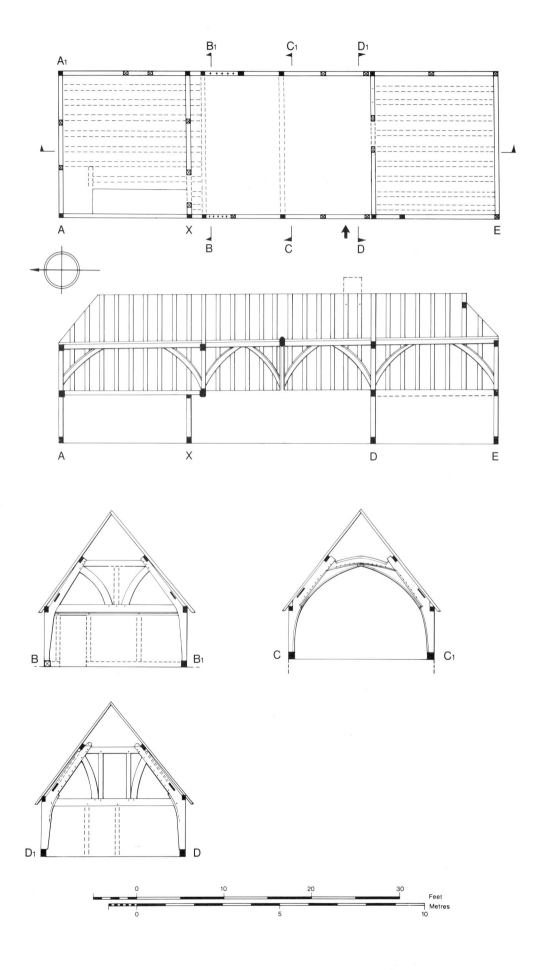

A₁

B₁   C₁   D₁

A   X   B   C   D   E

A   X   D   E

B   B₁

C   C₁

D₁   D

0   10   20   30   Feet
0   5   10   Metres

4

Park View, Tichborne

Grid Ref: 572305

A four-bay cruck house c.1450

Park View looking towards the north end of the hall.

This timber-framed hall house lies parallel to the village street on a small plot. According to a manorial survey of c.1560, however, it is probable that a small farm of about 30 acres went with the house at that time (H.R.O. Eccl. 155651).

The house is thatched. Visible from the outside are parts of the massive sill beams on which rest the cruck feet and intervening studs, making large square panels between sill and wall plate. Five pairs of cruck blades divide the house into four bays. Each blade is truncated above the collar. The crucks at D/ D′ have been reused from another building where they served as part of an open hall truss. Evidence for

this previous use is the spare tenons at the ends of the cruck blades, perhaps for a second collar or for an extension towards the apex jointed at the ends of the blades, and empty mortices indicated by peg holes for arch braces. The other crucks at Park View have no such spare tenons and were purposely carpentered for the present building.

There is no ridge piece and the roof is half-hipped at both ends. There are common rafters along the length of the house and side purlins rest on the back of the cruck blades. In each bay, pairs of wind braces rise from cruck to purlin.

The service bay (D-E) was originally floored with

Park View, Tichborne: a cruck-built house seen from the north east. (PMJC)

axial joists similar to those which survive in the parlour bay (A-B). Mortices for these joists can be found along the bressummer at D/D', but the joists were removed c.1968. There may never have been a stair opening in bay D-E since access to the loft was obviously intended between the collar and tie beams of truss D/D', where two studs make a rectangular entrance which was presumably reached by ladder from the hall. This entrance was originally open, since there are no stave holes or groove in the collar or tie beam to support a wattle wall. There is a gablet at the roof apex above the service bay and the rafters of both this bay and the hall (B-D) are heavily smoke-blackened. Thus smoke escaped through the entrance to the loft, but there is also evidence for a louvre in the pegholes in two pairs of rafters at the lower end of the hall.

The hall, which contains two roughly equal bays, has a handsome central truss (C/C') with a cambered collar and arch braces. The crucks, braces and collar are well finished and chamfered on both sides. At the lower end of the hall, pegholes and mortices in the wallplates provide evidence for the jambs of two opposing external doors, and for a bressummer perhaps for the screens of a cross passage. At the high end of the hall were small mullioned windows on either side and an internal jetty (X-B).

The parlour bay (A-B) retains good quality axial joists and part of the trimmer for the original stair opening, where there is now a modern staircase. There appears to be no framing for windows in the lofts at either end of the building and it is possible that they were originally unlit.

Probably in the 17th century, the hall was partly floored and a timber chimney inserted. This floor and remnants of the chimney were removed c.1983. Extensions to the north and west of the building were made in the 19th and 20th centuries. About 1968, the floors were excavated, the joists in the service bay removed and an enlarged dormer was made above the parlour.

Facing Page
Park View from the north east

5

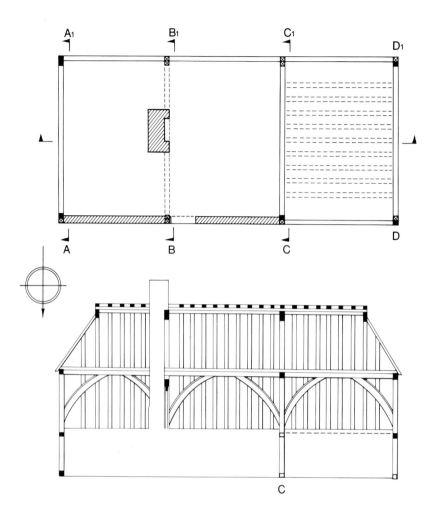

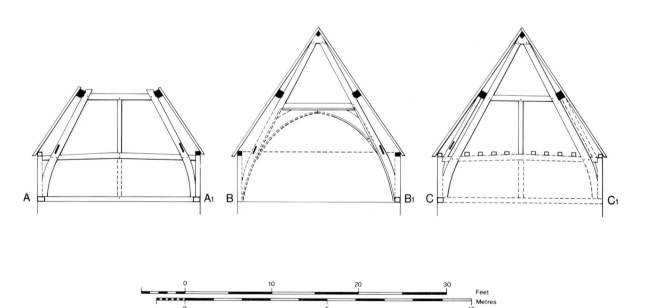

5
Embassy Cottage, Queen Street, Twyford
Grid Ref: SU 479244

A three-bay cruck house c.1450.

Embassy Cottage, Twyford: the north elevation. (EVR)

Embassy cottage lies back some 10 yards from the street and parallel to it. It is a three-bay house with four pairs of crucks. The roof is half-hipped at both ends, where the crucks are necessarily truncated just above the collars. On both sides of the central bay are full crucks yoked together beneath the ridge piece (type C: Alcock 1981, 7). There is a two-bay hall (A-C) and a floored bay, which was probably the parlour, at the western end.

It could be argued that Embassy Cottage may have had a small service bay beyond cross frame A/A', similar to the service bay at Little Thatches, Ashley (6). However, this is unlikely because there is no evidence for a doorway in A/A', nor for the projection of wall plates or sill beams beyond this crossframe.

The side purlins rest on the backs of the cruck blades. Curved wind braces descend from the purlins to the crucks, or (in the case of truss C/C') to a packing piece which rests on the spur or bressummer end. The hall truss B/B' is well finished with chamfered crucks, arch braces and collar. The original axial joists in bay C-D have been removed, but sawn off tenons for them can be seen in the bressummer at D/D'.

The ceiling in bay C-D has been raised, some of the original joists being re-used. The present arrangement of joists has been drawn on the plan, but originally there must have been a stair opening. The hall has been floored and a chimney inserted. Seventeenth or eighteenth century extensions adjoin both east and west ends of the house.

47

6

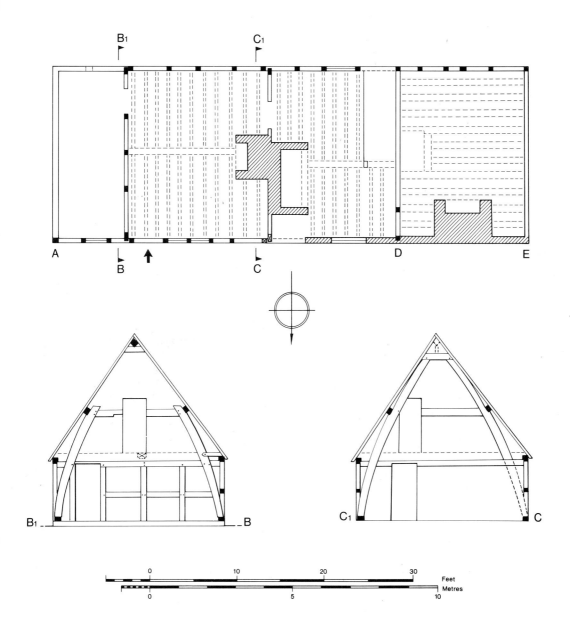

B₁   C₁

A

B

C   D   E

B₁   B   C₁   C

```
        0              10              20              30
                                                            Feet
                                                            Metres
        0                       5                       10
```

6
Little Thatches, Ashley

Grid Ref: SU 383311

A cruck house, c.1450

Little Thatches, Ashley from the west. (EVR)

This house stands right against the village street and parallel to it. It has always been thatched, since both the rafters and the underside of the thatch are smoke-blackened in bay B-C.

The house was probably built with three bays, the central bay B-C being an open hall. Bay D-E is probably an extension, but may possibly be a reconstruction of an original fourth bay. Bay A-B is only 7 feet 3 inches in length and seems to have been intended as a small service bay. It could be argued that the western end of the house originally ended in a half-hip at B/B' with no service bay, as at Embassy Cottage, Twyford (5). The truncated crucks at B/B' and the fact that the purlins do not extend into the service bay A-B, make this a possibility. However, we argue that bay A-B is an original feature of the house on the evidence of the doorway in crossframe B/B' and of the ridge piece which extends right up to B/B'. Furthermore, the wall plate and sill beam on the southern side of the house project past post B to the post at A.

There are full crucks at truss C/C', joined by a yoke beneath the ridge piece. The tie beam is halved into the crucks, and struts and rails form a small-panelled partition between tie and sill beams.

Truss D/D' is box framed at present, but the purlins which end at this truss are cut as if they were originally intended to be halved into cruck blades which have since been removed.

Bay A-B seems never to have been floored and in this respect is comparable to the small service bay at Riverside (2). The spine beam and transverse joists in Bay B-C have been inserted and the smoke-blackening on the rafters above suggests that this was originally a single bay open hall. The transverse joists in bay C-D probably replace original axial joists.

Bay D-E is box framed and the ridge is 5 feet 8 inches higher than the rest of the house, allowing the ridge piece from C-D to rest on the collar beam at D/D'. This would suggest that bay D-E was an addition of c.1600. However, it contains fine, medieval axial joists, which may have been moved from bay C-D when a chimney was inserted in that bay. In the twentieth century, an addition was made beyond A-A' obscuring the hipped roof.

49

7

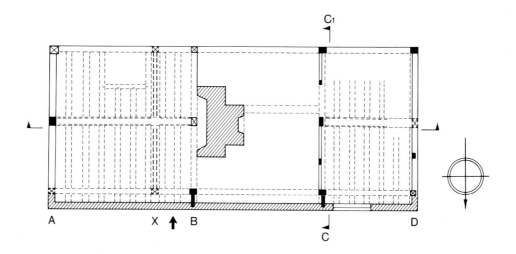

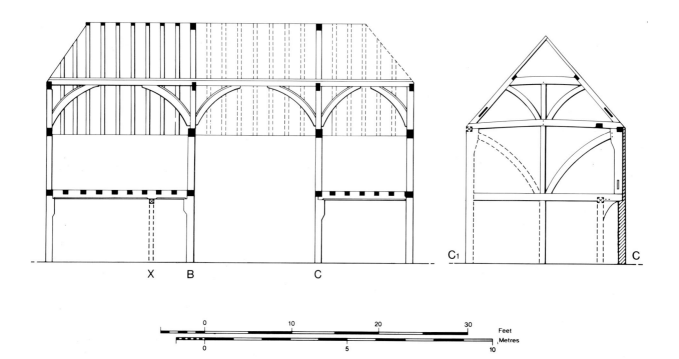

7
The Barracks, Wickham
Grid Ref: SU 574115
A three-bay Wealden house with a single bay hall c.1450.

The Barracks is the most complete example of a Wealden house in the area. It stands lengthwise along Bridge Street, Wickham.

There is a central single-bay hall with roof timbers blackened from an open fire. The front wall of the hall was removed when the later brick facing was added, so we have no information on the framing or the position of the hall window. Peg holes for mortices in the soffit of the flying wall plate indicate the position of two open or flying braces springing from the posts on the outside facade of the hall, a typical feature of the Wealden house. However, most of the eastern Wealdens have a secondary or inner plate behind the flying wall plate which marks the recessed front wall of the hall, as in the Hambledon example (9). There is no sign of this at the Barracks, nor at Alexandra House (8) in Wickham Square. However, in both the Wickham houses there is a stud behind the post halved into the braces of the cross frame (C/C'), which must represent the line of the recessed front wall of the hall. It is possible that an inner plate was simply lodged on top of the tie beam leaving no apparent trace after its removal (effectively reversed assembly). This is a flimsier method than would be necessary in a two bay hall where the weight of the roof on the tie beam would require normal assembly (Martin 1977-87, ii 54-56).

The passage is within the service bay (A-B) which is floored by means of a spine beam supported on jowled posts. A gap in the chamfers on the spine beam and a corresponding mortice in the side girt of the south wall give the position of the partition (X/X') on the east side of the passage, shown dotted on the long section. It would be normal to have an entrance from the street at the north end of the passage, and one giving access at the rear opposed to it. Similarly we would expect an opening to the passage from the hall, as for example at the Blue Boar (13), but here the details are obscured by the later insertion of a chimney.

There is evidence for a stair in the service bay, where a trimmer to the floor joists remains; and there could have been one in the corresponding position in the parlour bay, where the stairs are today.

The roof is half hipped at the east end and has undiminished principals with clasped purlins. There are curved windbraces in all bays. There are curved queen struts between tie and collar. Such a roof is typical of fifteenth century houses in Wickham, but would be quite out-of-place in the homeland of Wealden houses – Kent and Sussex – where crown post roofs are usual.

Some exterior framing is visible, especially on the first floor which, on the south side has curved braces to each bay with a central stud, similar to 81/82 Hursley (28).

All the timbers are well chosen and have heavy scantlings, making the Barracks an impressive and solid, if undecorated house, which may be relatively early. It is quite recognisable as a Wealden from the outside, even though the jetties have been underbuilt and the north wall of the hall extended and rebuilt in brick. A later property has been added to the west end, so the continuous roofline is deceptive. The brick chimney was inserted into the hall (with additional later flues) about 1600.

The north east side of the Barracks: the two jetties have been underbuilt in brick. (PMJC)

Facing page:
The north east side of the Barracks, Wickham.

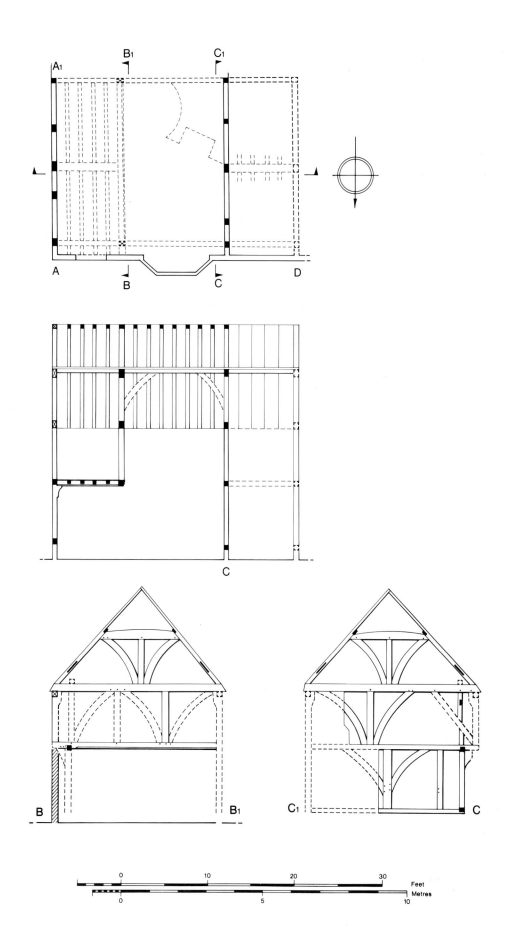

A₁ B₁ C₁

A B C D

C

B B₁ C₁ C

0   10   20   30   Feet
0   5   10 Metres

8

Alexandra House, Wickham

Grid Ref: SU 573114

A three-bay Wealden house with a half-floored hall, c.1450

Alexandra House, Wickham: A Wealden house now divided into two properties. The ridge line indicates the length of the original medieval building. (EVR)

Alexandra House stands on the south side of Wickham Square, lengthwise to the street. It occupies bays A-C of a three bay Wealden house, the third bay C-D being now a shop. Nothing can be seen of bay C-D inside the sweet shop, but from the outside the early roof line extends for about 7 feet, and is probably still visible in the attic, as the ends of windbraces in this part can be seen in Alexandra House.

Of the two bays of the medieval house that are visible, the back wall and front wall are missing, and some of the framing in the cross walls. The house was of three bays, of which the central bay was longer (11'6") than the end bays (7'). The two end bays were certainly jettied, the brackets supporting the missing jetty beam are still in position. In bay A-B, the joists (which may be replacements) supporting the upper floor are carried by a spine beam. Bays A-C formed a half-floored hall. The bressumer (B/B') is elaborately moulded on the side facing the open bay (B-C). Later alteration has removed the cross wall B/B' on the first floor but evidence for it survives in voided mortices in the bressumer and the soffit of the tie

beam. The short length of the open bay (B-C) is presumably here the reason for adding to its floor area the space below the chamber at the end.

The cross sections show that Alexandra House was originally a Wealden house like the Barracks (7), and it has the same constructional details with a stud behind the first floor posts halved into the braces of the cross walls, and an absence of any indication of an inner wall plate. In the reconstruction of the Barracks we have proposed a lodged plate above the tie, and this could be suggested here too.

The hall was floored over, perhaps late in the 17th century; a fragment of painting survived on the plaster between the joists. There is no trace of a chimney of this date. Most of the alterations belong to the late eighteenth century; the double fireplace and staircase, the extension at the back which must have been built at the same time, the corner fireplace in the upper east room and the cellar. The external appearance of the house is largely due to alterations in the early 19th century, when the facade was bricked up and the eaves line lifted.

9

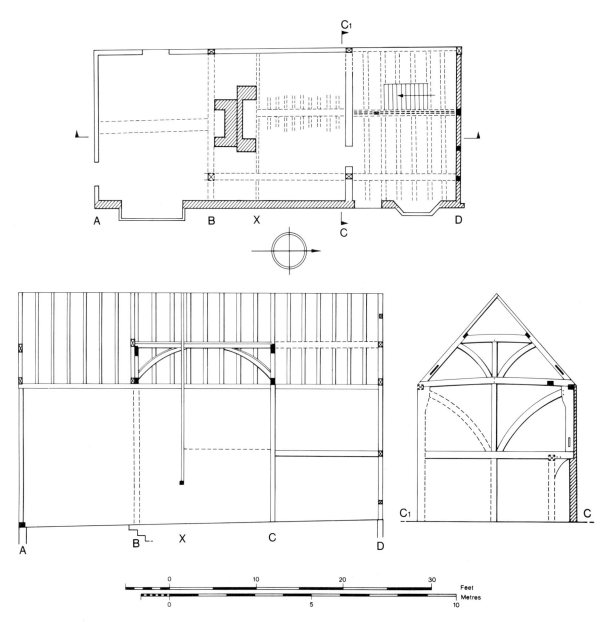

9

Nos. 3 and 4 High Street, Hambledon

Grid Ref: SU 646150

A Wealden house with single-bay hall and one surviving floored bay, c.1450.

The house stands on the west side of the High Street, lengthwise to the street. There are stone walls at the north end of the cellar of No.4 which may be residual from an earlier building. Although the house is much altered, the cross frames and roof trusses for the hall bay and the service bay survive. The service bay at the north end was divided lengthwise into two rooms as shown by the mortices in the spine beam. There is no surviving evidence for a passage or screens, or doorways to the hall. The floor joists in this north bay are scribed for the position of the jetty beam and there is in the bressummer of truss C the characteristic mortice for the jowled jetty support post.

At the south end, the existing bay (A-B) is of seventeenth century date, and it is likely that this replaced an earlier parlour bay. There is no sign of weathering on the south side of the hall cross frame, so probably the building was not simply of two bays but was a full Wealden.

The hall has both an inner and a flying wall plate as evidence for the Wealden form. The inner plate has mortice evidence for a mullioned window. This plate is morticed into the tie beams at each end of the hall, but whether it was supported by a stud as well is not clear as the soffit of the tie is concealed. The post at C has evidence for one of a pair of flying braces to the outer plate on the outside of the hall, characteristic of Wealden houses such as The Yeoman's House, Bignor, Sussex or Bayleaf at Singleton.

The roof has diminished principal rafters clasping side purlins. There are curved raking struts and curved windbraces.

Perhaps in the sixteenth century, the open hall was converted by the insertion of a nailed-in truss to form a smoke bay, which survives in good condition at attic level heavily smoke blackened. This was made redundant by a brick chimney of early seventeenth century date, perhaps put in at the time the southern

Nos 3-4 High Street, Hambledon: the white painted brick work with its decorative string course presents an eighteenth century appearance, concealing the medieval framing within. (PMJC)

bay was rebuilt. In the seventeenth century the front of the house facing the street was bricked up, with a decorative string course with egg-and-dart moulding exactly corresponding to the length of the hall. Further brickwork was added in the eighteenth century completely concealing the timber frame. An outshut was built at the rear together with various piecemeal additions.

The landholdings around High Street (then North Street) in 1552 have been analysed and show that while most properties were held copyhold this house was owned freehold by Anthony Uvedale esquire of the well-known Hampshire family. His widowed mother held one of the houses at the bottom of the street beside the Manor House. (HRO. Eccles 1568819:6/10. Col. K. Roberts, pers.comm).

From 1910 until the mid-sixties the south part was a butcher's shop.

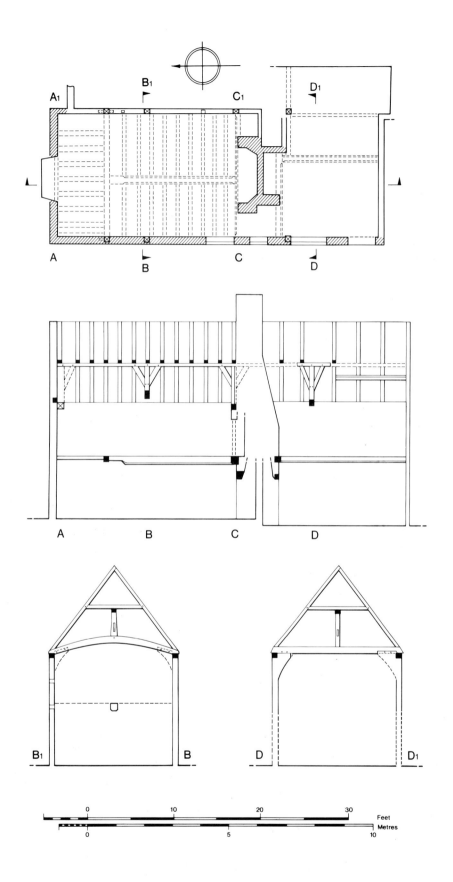

Feet
Metres

10

Moysents, Bishops Waltham

House with two-bay hall and crown post roof c.1350.

Moysents represents a rare survival in the area of a domestic hall with a crown post roof, and possibly an end gallery.

This house, now in dual ownership, stands on a corner plot between Bank Street (originally French Street) and Basingwell Street, its long side to Basingwell Street. It may be identified with the property belonging to John Burhunte in 1464, a tiler who held of the Bishop of Winchester "one messuage – where Moysents lived and afterwards John Cokker – situated next to the cottage which belonged to Thomas Ludgate and abutting in length the cottage of John Innehave in the street called Frenchstrete and lying upon the corner of the lane called Basingwell Lane..." (HRO Eccles 2 158819 10/10; Mr T. Harvey, pers.comm).

We interpret the plan of the house as having a hall of two bays, (A-C), with a gallery at the north end where the house was possibly jettied onto Bank Street, and a floored bay (C-D-?) with an open truss (D/D') in the chamber above. However, the visible details of construction are often insufficient or ambiguous.

The hall truss B/B' has a cambered tie beam surmounted by a short square sectioned crown post, braced to the collar purlin with straight braces. The tie and common rafter are both scribed as truss II. The posts at B/B' had no jowls but were the same depth as the wall plates into which they were morticed in the manner of studs. The tie is rather inadequately anchored to the plate by means of a single-sided dovetail, and there is a voided mortice for a short brace or bracket, rather like a separately pegged jowl. The constructional relationship of the tie beam and wall plate suggest an early date (Hewett 1980, 273).

At the north end of the hall, peg holes in the collar purlin indicate the position of a crown post at the gable end (scribed truss I). At this end there appears to have been an open gallery 4' 6" wide with flat-laid medieval joists housed in a bressumer. At the south end of the hall one post (C') survives with neither jowl nor brace. The straight tie beam at C/C', (scribed III) supports a crown post. There are no positive indications – such as peg holes – that there was a partition beneath the tie, nor that the bay beyond was floored, but the insertion of the chimney stack has obscured some evidence. D/D' seems to be an intermediate open truss perhaps for an upper floor chamber. It has a straight tie beam with a crown post. On either side of this crown post, the collar purlin has been sawn through for the insertion of the stack to the

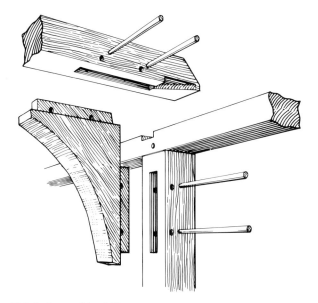

Detail of assembly at B'.

The crown post over the central hall truss. (JRB)

59

Renamed Moysents after a medieval owner, this house was photographed in 1973, shortly after Lock's fish shop vacated the building (JRB).

north, and for the rebuilding of the roof with side purlins on the south side. However there is evidence that this crown post is of slightly later date than the others. Unlike those in the hall, it is of pit-sawn timber and slightly different in form; it is not pegged into the tie beam; it has no truss numbering marked on it; and the posts supporting the tie beam are jowled. These two bays may represent an addition to the hall, or a rebuild of an existing bay; in neither case is it possible to establish the total length of the building because of rebuilding at the south end.

The east wall of the house retains its original wall plate, side girt and some studs. At first floor level there were long curved tension braces reaching from the side girt to the central post of the hall truss.

Post-medieval alterations to the house included a large timber-framed extension to the east, along Bank Street. A chimney stack was inserted in the bay south of the hall, and the hall was floored over by introducing a spine beam, neatly chamfered and stopped, but clumsily fitted into the existing gallery bressumer. The walls on the street frontages were completely rebuilt in brick.

11

Boots the Chemist, 35 High Street, Winchester

Grid Ref: SU 482294

Fragments of a Wealden house, circa 1350 – 1400.

Two bays, or partial bays (8ft and 9ft long) of the roof of a Wealden house survive in this building. The end trusses are missing but the central hall truss with a crown post roof is in position (section M/M'). This Wealden house was apparently set back from the street and parallel to it. It was later extended to the present frontage. No. 34 was built up against the east end of the hall and probably replaced the chambered bay here.

The roof combines two structural types which may be contemporary or sequential (section M/M'). The tie beam clearly belongs to a Wealden building because it is cantilevered over the post M to form the middle truss of the typical recessed hall. There are ashlar pieces to the inner wall plate. The second, outer or flying wall plate is missing but the tie has an exposed dovetail which indicates its position. The post bears two mortices: one for a brace to the tie and another for a diagonal strut between the brace and the jowl of the post.

The crown post is tall, plain, undecorated and square in section. It supports a collar purlin which is chamfered on the lower arrises. The collars are all tenoned into the rafters. The crown post has curved braces (C_2/C) to the collar purlin (but not to the collars) and tension braces to the tie beam.

Halved around the crown post immediately above the brace to the collar purlin, there is a second, lower collar. This is tenoned into diminished principals and clasps side purlins which have wind braces pegged to the underside (M/M').

Combined in one roof we therefore have a crown post, trussed rafter roof and a side purlin roof. It is possible that the side purlins are an adaptation of the original crown post structure, perhaps for added stability. If this is the case, the original roof may be as early as the fourteenth century, as suggested by the height of the crown post (10ft) and the strutted brace, seen by Mercer (1975, 81) as an early feature.

On the other hand, it is difficult to see how and why the adaptation was made. Very considerable skill would have been required to insert principal rafters in the place of common rafters in the main truss; and to fit the two collars, the lower one into complex bracing. Thus it is possible that the whole roof was constructed in one build as a hybrid form between the crown post trussed rafter roof and the more up-to-date side purlin roof. Hampshire has examples of houses with both kinds of roof. In a county where side purlin roofs apparently developed early and became so popular, it does not seem so extraordinary that an experimental hybrid roof should occur.

In York there are three examples of roofs with crown posts associated with side purlins which are clasped by raking struts, without the lower collar seen at Winchester. The earliest is thought to date from circa 1320, the latest (111 Walmgate) on documentary evidence was built in 1396 (Short 1980 119, 133).

11 & 12

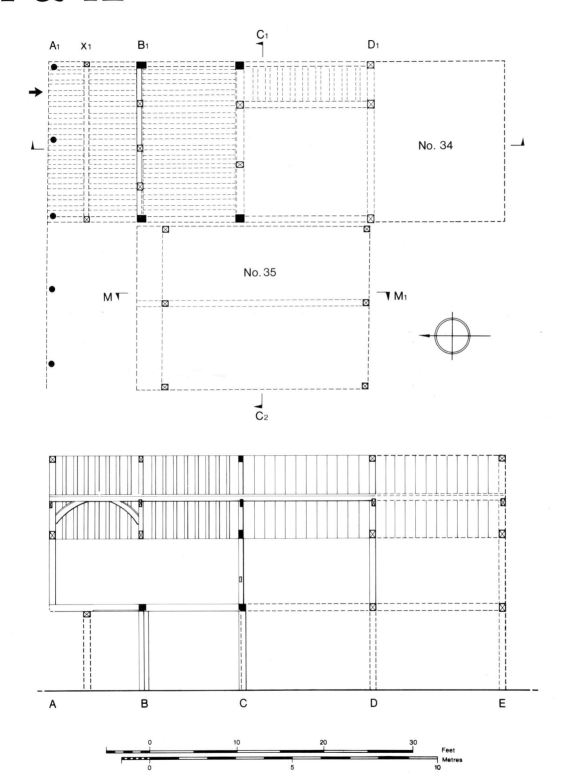

11 & 12

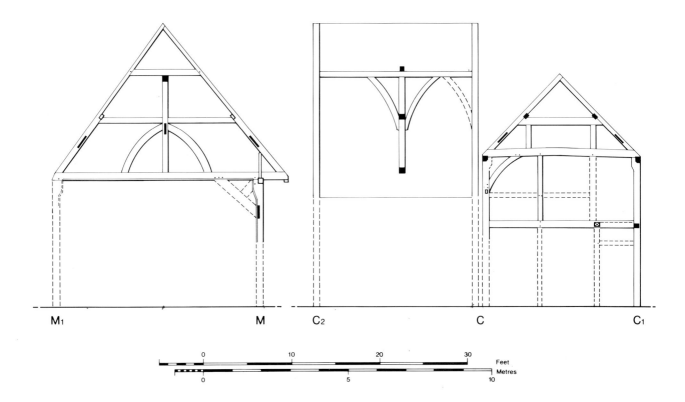

M₁   M   C₂   C   C₁

Feet

Metres

Nos 33-34 High Street, Winchester: Two medieval shops with
barge boards of the same design, overlooking the Pentice. (PMJC)

12

33 and 34 High Street, Winchester

Grid Ref: SU 482294

Two jettied shops with galleried halls c.1480

These two properties stand end on to Winchester High Street abutting the east end of the Wealden hall at No. 35 (11) (only No,34 is ilustrated here). Mos. 33 and 34 share a party wall and their plans were identical. They both have chamfered and cusped bargeboards to the same design. Both originally had a rather deep jetty oversailing the street, which was later supported by wooden columns, probably in the early eighteenth century. Perhaps at the same time the whole of the front wall and the first bay of each building was cut away to provide the pedestrian walk-way that is now known as the 'Pentice'. However, the evidence for the jetty bressumer (X/X') survives, and was observed during alterations in 1980 and 1987. This demonstrates that there was a short room or enclosed space (X-B) 5'6" long, floored with chamfered joists in the space now occupied by the Pentice. This was closed off from the main room (B-C) which was 10'6" long. Behind this room was an open hall (C-D) 14' long.

Unfortunately the whole of the roof over the hall of No.34 was destroyed during seventeenth-century building alterations, but it seems likely that this was a single-bay hall. Along its eastern wall was a gallery supported on a bressumer, the mortices for which survive in the cross beam (section C/C'). Access to the two-bayed first floor room at the north end of the house would have been along the gallery, where there is evidence for a doorway. There were indications before the 1980 alterations that there had been a further bay south of the hall.

Number 33, examined prior to alteration in 1987 by the RCHME, retained the whole of the hall roof, which had windbraces and an intermediate truss with a simple collar. The ground floor of the hall had been severely damaged and the cross beams replaced with steel RSJs. However, there was evidence for a gallery in the same position as that in No. 34. It was supported on a gallery bressumer which, although recently severed from the rest of the timber frame, appears to be in its original position. It is chamfered on both faces, stopping at mortices at each end which probably held studs forming two short speres. So a screened passage was created on the ground floor below the gallery. On the first floor, the gallery gave access to a doorway (with door jamb and mortice for doorhead surviving) leading to two single-bay front rooms. Nothing survived of a service room to the south, and there was some

evidence, in the weathering on the south side of the hall roof, that there had been no further bays. The first floor front room was originally divided into two (unlike that in No. 34), and the upper part of the frame was closed off as a partition.

The unusual feature of this pair of buildings is the extra rather short front room (X-B) which may have been used as a shop, or stall, perhaps with large openings which could be closed with shutters at night, protected by the deep overhang of the jetty. This feature, with variations, was shared by a group of adjacent buildings and may have been what was referred to as the 'Pentice' throughout the sixteenth century and as early as the fourteenth (Keene 1985, 561). The well-finished room (B-C) behind the shop could have been a show room for goods or the merchant's private parlour, with the hall and service rooms behind.

There was a similar arrangement at the Cock, Thaxted, Essex (Stenning 1985, 35) which also had a galleried hall behind the shop, end on to the street. However the Cock was significantly different in that it lacked a parlour or similar room behind the shop and was provided with a passage connecting the street with the hall; a passage in this position seems to be characteristic of many other medieval shops but cannot be proven in the case of No. 33 and 34. The property at 58 French Street, Southampton (Faulkener 1975, 104) has a galleried hall with a shop beneath a deep jetty supported on posts like the pentice: the passage up to and through the hall is clearly marked.

A brick chimney stack was inserted into the hall of No. 34 with a fireplace on the first floor with carved chalk-cut jambs. This may have been the chimney which Robert Hodson was required to build along with a loft (?attic) as a condition of his 50 year lease in 1554. (Keene 1985, 559) Certainly by the seventeenth century the hall was floored and the room above was panelled throughout in oak. In 1871 the lease of no. 34 was taken up by Mr T. Foster who opened a tobacconist's shop and remodelled the interior. The fittings were removed to the City Museum in 1980 when the shop's interior was rebuilt and the timber frame revealed once more.

Number 33 has suffered from recent interior alterations, but is distinguished in nineteenth century photographs by its semi circular bay window.

13

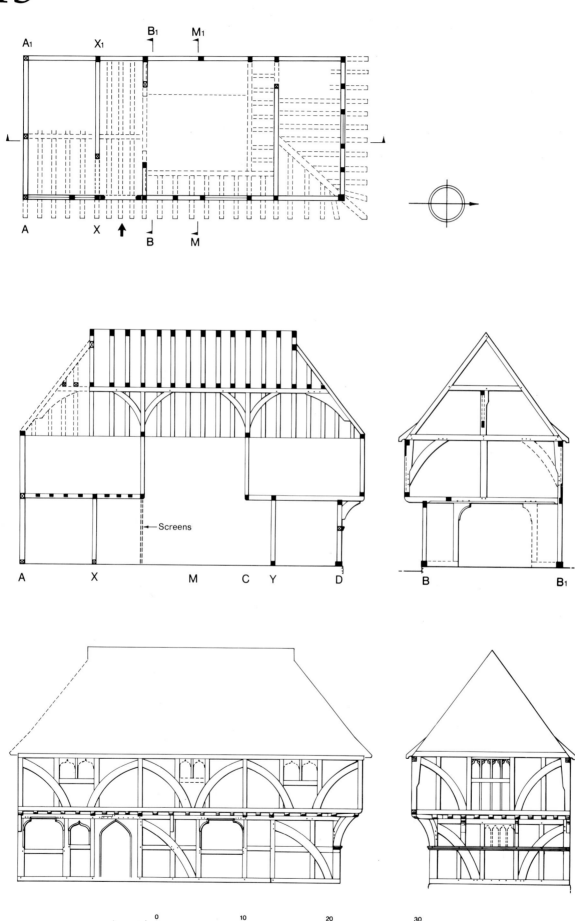

A₁   X₁   B₁   M₁

A   X   B   M

Screens

A   X   M   C   Y   D

B   B₁

0   10   20   30   Feet
0   5   10   Metres

13

The Blue Boar, St. John's Street, Winchester

Grid Ref: SU 487295

A galleried hall house of three bays c. 1380

This house is situated at the corner of St. John's Street and Blue Boar Hill, a key position between the city of Winchester and the site of the medieval St. Giles's Fair. The house was called "Late Blue Boar Inn" in 1774 (Keene 1985, 1067).

The interpretation of this house presents particular difficulty in that it was seriously damaged in 1968. Subsequent restoration seems to have been in general restrained and accurate, on the evidence both of existing framing and of photographs taken during restoration (PWCM 14099-14126).

This is a three-bay hall house with a jettied northern end and a continuous jetty along the eastern side. It contains a service bay with cross passage, a hall, and a parlour bay. Before restoration, the roof was fully hipped at both ends (Warren, 1903, 12). The roof has collars to each pair of common rafters and braces spring from the crown posts to the collar purlin. Although the roof has been largely renewed, these features would seem to be original (PWCM 14100).

The wall framing has large panels with tension braces on both floors. The door and window frames on the ground floor pre-date the restoration of 1968 (PWCM 14123 and 14126) and appear to be original, since they are incorporated into the structure of the house. The size of the large windows and their lack of

Interior of the hall of the Blue Boar, looking towards the screens, with the internal gallery reconstructed on the left. (PMJC)

mullions suggest that the house was planned as a shop.

The first floor window openings appear to be in their original positions, although the ogee window heads and mullions on the east elevation are probably replacements. On the north elevation the window of four trefoiled lights and the moulded string course pre-date the restoration of 1968. A 14th century date has been suggested for both features (Wood 1965, 224). However there is some doubt as to whether the window is in its original position.

The continuous jetty outside the hall is balanced by a parallel, gallery bressumer within the hall, which carries the jetty joists (section M/M'). This bressumer, with the joists, creates an internal gallery along the eastern wall of the hall, approximately four feet wide. However, it is unlikely that this gallery provided access across the hall between first floor rooms since it is blocked by large braces at either end. Nor is there any framing for a handrail to prevent those standing on the gallery from toppling down

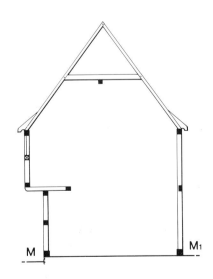

M   M₁

The Blue Boar from the east. (PMJC)

into the hall. Although the gallery bressumer was renewed in 1968, the original was faithfully copied (PWCM 14108; Mr J. Ashby, builder, pers. comm.). Apart from photographic and verbal evidence, there are mortices in the bressumers of both cross frames to receive it. (Section B/B')

The gallery on the west side of the hall is unconvincingly related to the original framing of the building and may have been a feature created during the restoration of 1968 in order to provide access to first floor rooms. To achieve this end, doorways were made beneath the tie beams where arch braces would originally have blocked access. Because of the dubious nature of this gallery, it has been indicated as a single dotted line on the plan.

The joists at the parlour end are partly renewed and at the service end partly obscured, so the evidence for stairs may have been destroyed. However, there must have been stair openings in both end bays, if the possibility of access through a hall gallery is discounted.

The hall has an internal jetty at the parlour end and a chamfered bressumer above the screens at the service end. One screen survives with an original post and bracket forming a shouldered archway (PWCM 14123).

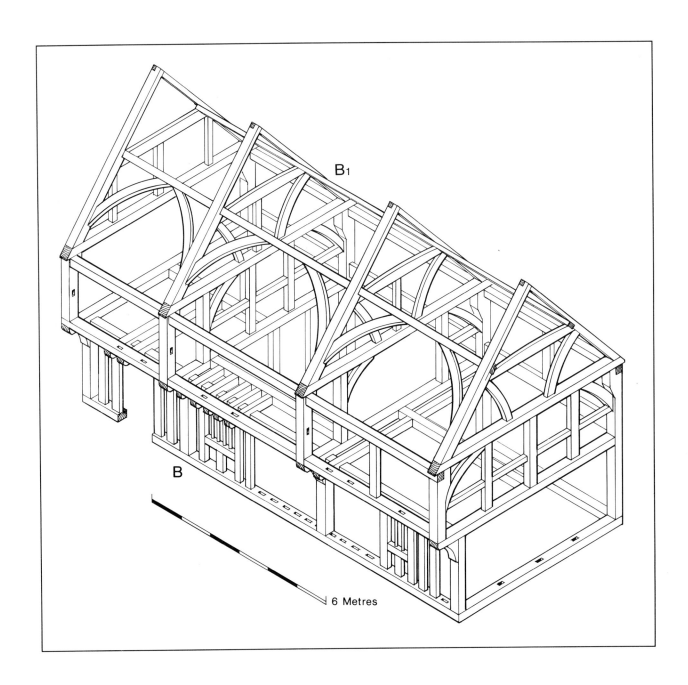

B₁

B

6 Metres

The Curio Shop, Wickham in 1968. (EL)

14
The Curio Shop, Wickham
Grid Ref: SU 572114

A galleried hall house of three bays. c.1470

This house (now called Knockers Wine Bar) was published in detail elsewhere (Lewis 1979, 203) but the cross section is shown here for comparison with the galleried halls at the Blue Boar, Winchester (13), and The Crease, Micheldever (16). The house stands lengthwise to the street on the west side of the Square. The section B/B' shows a closed bay at the west end of the hall. There is a mortice for an axial bressumer which supports the gallery along the jetty, and opposed doorways onto the gallery give access from the two upper chambers. Only one staircase would be needed and was probably in the western bay.

In character and craftsmanship the house is very close to the two Wealdens in Wickham – the Barracks (7) and Alexandra House (8) – and might be seen as a direct derivation from the Wealden form.

The sawn off joists of the hall gallery which gave access to an upper chamber through a door way. (JRB)

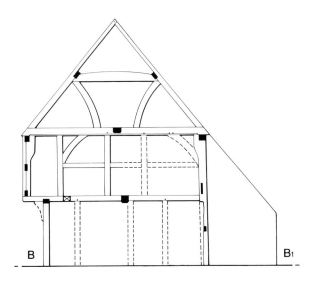

15

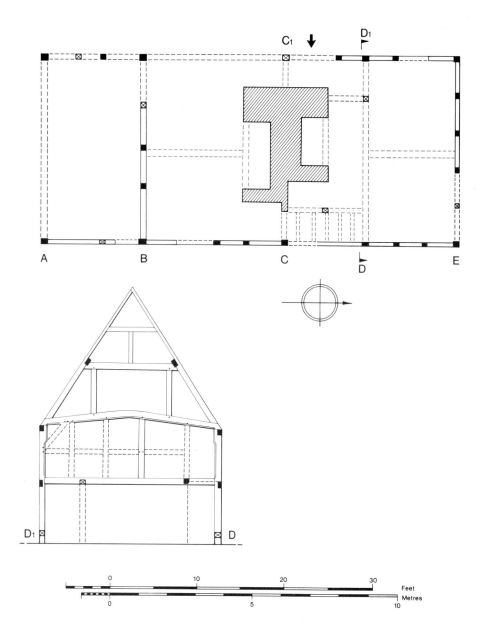

15
Perry's Acre, Micheldever
Grid Ref: SU 514390

A four-bay house with a galleried hall, c.1550

Perry's Acre, Micheldever from the east. The framing for the smoke bay can be seen below the chimney. (EVR)

This house stands back some ten yards from the east of the small village green. It is thatched and the exterior wall framing is formed with small panels and straight braces.

Internally, the most interesting feature is a gallery, 8ft. 3 inches in length, which crosses the east side of the open hall bay (C-D) at first floor level. The cross-frame at D/D' shows that this gallery is an original feature and not an addition, for it leads to a neatly framed doorway beside post D. This has always been an open doorway because there are no stave holes in the soffit of the tie beam at this point and there is no mortice for a brace in post D to match the brace at post D'. Stave holes and a void mortice in the soffit of the gallery beam indicate a partition to create a passage way beneath the gallery, possibly to create a heck, or partition for a baffle entry (opposite the doorway marked on the plan). Oddly, there appears to be no mortice in the soffit of the bressumer D/D' to mark the end of the partition.

The soffit of the bressumer D/D' has only one mortice for a stud about 4 feet from post D'. A bressumer running from this mortice towards C/C' may mark the line of a heck, or partition, screening the hall from an external door (suggested plan). The soffit of the bressumer at D/D' is otherwise unmarked which suggests that bays C-D and D-E have never been partitioned at ground floor level, and consequently would have formed a half-floored hall. Bay C-D has heavy soot-blackening on cross frames and rafters and was thus originally open to the roof. Its length (only 8ft 3 inches) leaves limited space for a hall and this alone would argue the need to join it with bay D-E at ground floor level to create an adequate living area. The same point can be made with regard to the half-floored hall at Monks Rest, Littleton (24).

Bays A-B, B-C and D-E have always been floored. The house has been extended at both north and south ends and a chimney has been inserted in the smoke bay area of the hall.

16

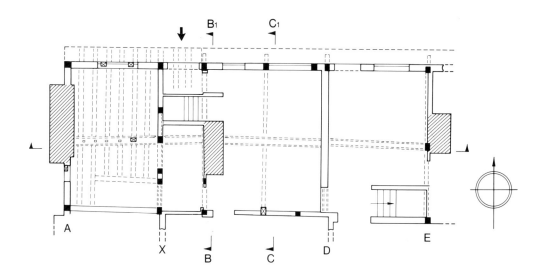

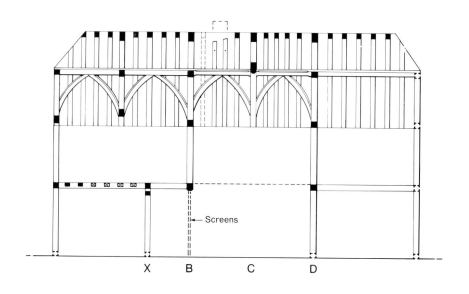

Screens

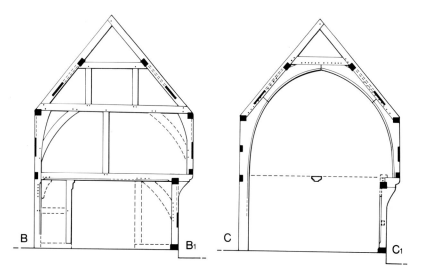

16
The Crease, Micheldever
Grid Ref: SU 514390

A four-bay continuous jetty hall house c.1475

This house stands on a bank above a road junction in the centre of the village. It has a continuous jetty along the north elevation, facing the road. Large curved braces form a striking feature of both north and west elevations.

The medieval house is of four bays, including a hall in two bays. This has a most unusual central truss resembling a jointed cruck (C/C'). On the south side the cruck is the full height of the wall, while on the north side the foot of the cruck is seated on the jetty and so is only the height of the first floor. The cruck continues above the wall plate and is pegged into the principal rafter and into an arch brace. This arch brace is also pegged along its length into the principal rafter and then into the collar. The purlins are clasped below the collar. All these features, including the tightly-curved wind braces, are very finely made and the undersides are chamfered.

Diamond-shaped mortices in the soffit of the wallplate show that a hall window extended between posts C and D high up in the south wall. Beneath the jetty on the northern side of the hall was a large window. Mortices for brackets suggest that this window was similar to the large ground floor windows at the Blue Boar, Winchester (13) which have consequently been the pattern adopted for the external reconstruction of the Crease. Above this window and on the inside of the hall is a shutter groove 8ft 6ins long which is attached to the jetty beam with large-headed iron nails of medieval type. There are pegholes for a corresponding shutter groove at sill level on the post and stud on either side of the window. This shutter groove is a secondary feature.

At the east end of the hall is a closed truss. This conforms more closely to local building tradition, having large curved braces to the tie beam and straight queen struts between the collar and tie. East of this closed truss is a small floored bay (D-E) with a spine beam supported at the east end by a jowled post. The joists are concealed. This room was probably the parlour.

To the west of the hall there was an overshot screens passage (X-B) with asymmetrical speres at either end (B/B'), leading to the front door facing the road. The chamfered door head and jambs survive. Dividing the passage from the service room is a partition wall (X/X') with three doorways; two are placed on either side of a central chamfered jamb and led to the

The hall truss of The Crease, Micheldever (16) has a jointed cruck resting on an internal gallery. The rest of the house is of box frame construction. (PMJC)

A view of the hall truss on the south side. (PMJC)

buttery and pantry in the conventional way. The spine beam in the service has voided mortices indicating an original partition. The third doorway probably gave access to a stair. Above is a large chamber spanned by an intermediate truss with a chamfered and gracefully cambered tie beam.

We interpret the building as an open hall with a very narrow gallery the width of the jetty but without joists (see reconstruction drawing). This joistless gallery must have been mainly decorative, or perhaps housed some shutter fixtures; on the outside it would have been finished perhaps by coving. The chamfer stop on the bressumer (section B/B') confirms that the jetty was an integral feature, and not, as might be suggested, an inserted late feature. It is thus a distinct variant on the galleries at the Blue Boar (13) and Curio Shop (14).

An alternative interpretation is that the hall was floored from the beginning, either wholly or between the spine beam and jetty. To counter this, we would argue that the principal joist was clearly not intended to extend beyond the wall post into the room. The illustration shows that an extended nib at the top of the wall post (C') clamps the principal joist securely in position. This nib would effectively block any extension of the principal joist into the room. Furthermore there is no seating for a principal joist on the full cruck (C), which has continuous chamfers. Finally the roof is very well sooted and there is evidence for a louvre at the western end of the hall as shown in the peg holes in two pairs of rafters (long section).

A chimney was inserted in the cross passage and the hall floored over c.1600. At about the same time, a single-bay, jettied extension was added to the eastern end of the house. A 17th century timber-framed house of three and a half bays is linked at right angles to the south side of the service bay.

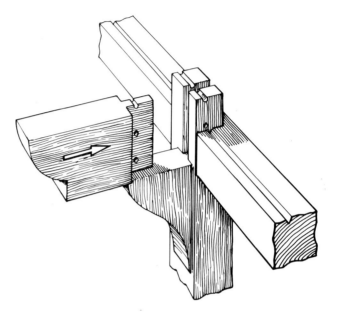

Detail of assembly at C' as seen from outside the building.

The hall looking west towards the screens.

The Crease from the north west. (PMJC)

Facing page:
The Crease from the north west.

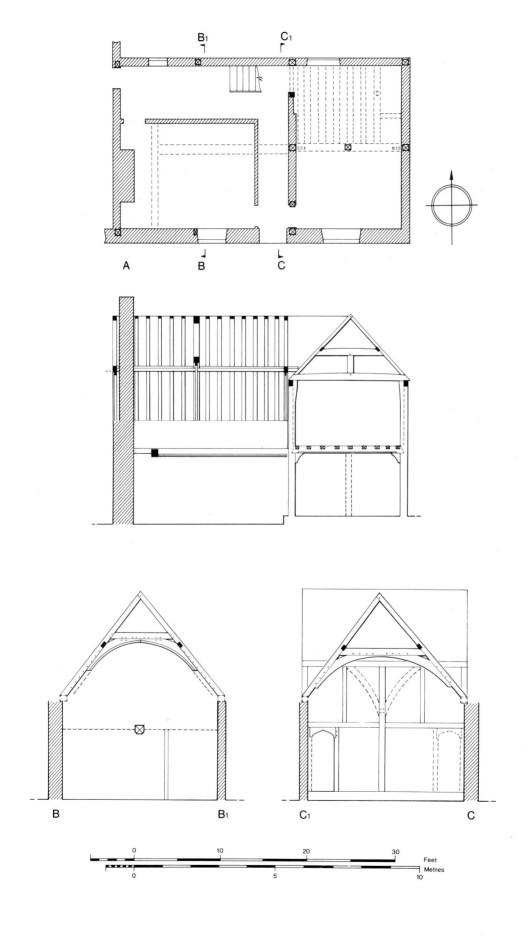

A   B   C

B₁   C₁

Feet
Metres

17

Gable House, Bank Street, Bishop's Waltham

Grid Ref: SU 554176

A two-bay open hall of about 1430 with a cross wing.

Gable House, Bishops Waltham when it was still the home of Bullock's Shop about 1914. The cross wing is concealed behind the near gable. (JRB)

Heavily disguised by a Victorian brick frontage, Gable House stands lengthwise along Bank Street, one of the medieval streets of Bishop's Waltham. Of the hall, three trusses survive (A,B,C). All of them are 'open' in the sense that there is no contemporary framing beneath the collars, which are arch braced. The centre truss is, however, different from the other two in having a higher collar and heavy principals into which the side purlins are butted. The moulding of the braces forms a double ogee profile (fig. 5.6) and the braces are fixed to the collar in part by means of 'free' tenons, loose blocks which are pegged into both the collar and the brace. The other two trusses have no mouldings and clasped purlins. The truss at the west end (A/A') has wattle and daub above the collar, much sooted. The truss at the eastern end (C/C') has no infill but the top of the collar is grooved. It seems therefore that both these trusses were originally closed at least above collar

level, and the curved braces are really decorative elements to the end walls, as can be seen on high status buildings, usually of stone, such as St. Cross Hospital, Winchester. So the hall had two bays and a moulded central truss.

The original floored bay at the west end is missing. The wall at the west end of the hall is obscured by modern brickwork, although the present land plot extends westwards and a shop was added at this end in the 19th century perhaps on the site of an earlier structure. The cross wing at the east end of the hall is separately framed; the hall purlins protrude 2ft into the roof space and this feature is compatible with either a contemporary or a later replacement cross wing.

The cross wing has two storeys, and is apparently divided on the ground floor by a partition wall into two rooms each opening into the hall. The doorway in the north room has an arched door head. There is evidence of a stair in the north room where there is a gap in the joists. The position of the doorway suggests this room was a parlour although the partition would support the idea of its function as a divided service bay.

The side purlin roof of the hall may be an early example; the moulding of the braces is similar to those at St. Cross Hospital (Hewett 1980, 312) though it occurs throughout the fifteenth century. The free tenons also appear to be an early trait (Hewett 1980, 176). There are no wind braces.

The roof of the cross wing is of lighter construction than that of the hall; the central truss has a short middle strut between tie and collar, and clasped purlins. This is a standard roof type in the area during the 15th and 16th centuries.

The hall was floored over with a spine beam and cross beam probably in the early seventeenth century. The evidence of this cross beam at the west end of the hall and the comparatively late and small chimney stack suggests that there was a timber chimney inserted into the east end of the hall when it was floored. The main alterations date from the late nineteenth century when the facade was rebuilt in brick and the house extended to the west.

18

Tudor House, East Meon

Grid Ref: SU678222

A hall truss c.1375

Tudor House is an L-shaped building which stands on the corner of The Cross and Workhouse Lane, East Meon. One truss survives from a medieval house which runs alongside Workhouse Lane. The dimensions of this building cannot be ascertained because the structures on either side of the medieval truss have been completely rebuilt, while remaining in the same east-west alignment.

The surviving truss is soot-blackened on both faces and was thus internal to a hall of two or more bays. Both collar and tie are steeply cambered and the tie and surviving post are deeply chamfered. An elegant brace joins tie and post. The most striking features of the truss are the cusped and chamfered arch braces, the two lower cusps having triangular recessed spandrels. On the back of the arch braces are pegholes and mortices for flying tenons to the original principals. The present principals and purlins are secondary.

Although little survives of the original building, there is nothing to suggest that this hall truss has been transferred from elsewhere. There are no signs of re-assembly and the north wall plate and post are in situ. Later framing has been built up to the truss on both sides, so that it is a fossil within a later

structure rather than an essential part of it. A bressumer below the tie beam (indicated by broken lines in the section) supports a floor which was inserted into the eastern bay of the hall in the late 16th century. Probably at the same time, a wattle and daub wall was applied to the western face of the hall truss. Remnants of this wall are now heavily sooted, suggesting that the wall's purpose was to create a smoke bay in the western part of the hall.

The combination of a tie beam and cusping on the arch braces in an open hall truss is reminiscent of the roof of the refectory at Great Malvern Priory now demolished, (Smith 1958, 126) and the building at Church Farm, Lewknor, Oxfordshire (Mercer 1975, 194) both of fourteenth century date. A recent survey (Alcock *et al* 1984, 47-55) lists further examples of these open truss tie beams.

According to documentary evidence, the Court House (40) was the only manorial house in East Meon. Thus, in spite of the relative pretension of the design at Tudor House and the sophisticated carving of the cusps, it seems that we must rule out a manorial status for the building. The small dimensions of the truss might argue a wealthy yeoman status.

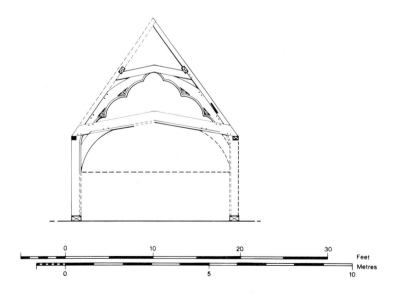

```
0            10           20          30
                                            Feet
                                            Metres
0                      5                10
```

19

Littleton Manor, Littleton

Grid Ref: SU 453328

A large timber-framed house with a central two-bay hall, c.1500

Littleton Manor looking from the north. The service bay is on the left. (JRB)

Both the name and size of this building proclaim its relatively high status. The long section shows that it is divided lengthwise into 3 large bays, each subdivided by intermediate trusses.

The original west end wall A/A' remains with its framing exposed. It is of close studding, infilled with knapped or surfaced flints and the surface of the timber shows signs of weathering. Peg holes along the wall plate on the northern elevation of the hall indicate close studding with curved braces on the first floor. The rest of the framework of the walls is concealed, along with any indications of original openings.

The bays are arranged with the parlour bay at the west end, floored with heavy joists. The chamber above has an exposed central open truss with collar and chamfered purlins.

At the high end of the hall (B/B') the door leading to the parlour survives and there is a handsome moulded cross beam (fig. 5.3). The cross beam at the lower end of the hall (D/D') is also moulded but

83

19

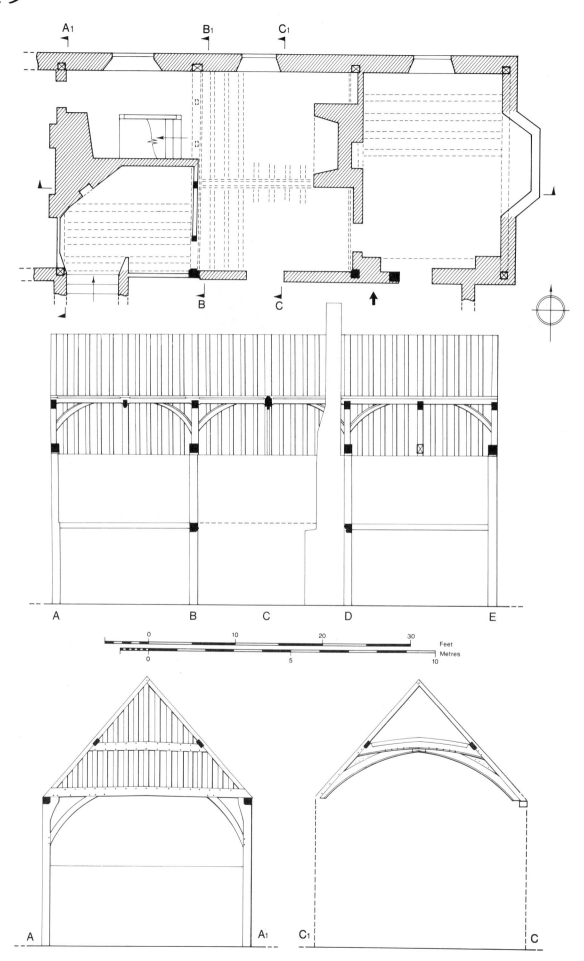

A₁ B₁ C₁

B

C

A   B   C   D   E

```
0          10          20          30        Feet
0              5                    10    Metres
```

A   A₁   C₁   C

Arch-braced collar over the hall at Littleton Manor. (JRB)

bears no visible pegholes for ground floor framing. The limited evidence suggests that screens were positioned below crossbeam D/D' and that posts D and X mark either side of a cross passage contained within the service bay (D-E).

The hall has a fine arch brace collar roof with the spandrels infilled in oak, pinned with iron nails (C/C'). There are undiminished principals with clasped purlins. The collar is chamfered at the top to a depth of 6 inches to emphasise the curve and give lightness – as at Park View, Tichborne (4). The braces and principals are also chamfered, and there is a very simple stop at the springing at the top of the wall.

Over the service bay to the east, the chamber is divided by a closed truss above the tie beam. The soffit of the tie beam shows no signs of a dividing wall on the first floor, but it may have been cut and trimmed at a later date, deleting the mortices. None

of the roof timbers in the service bay are chamfered, though the quality of the work is good throughout. The east end wall (E/E') is in fragmentary condition, but enough survives to show that it was originally close-studded and gabled like the west end.

A stone fireplace was inserted into the hall, perhaps in the later sixteenth century. The chimney was rebuilt later in brick, and the lintel replaced. The heavily moulded spine beam is inserted and has no stops. The parlour was divided in two and an oak stair inserted. It has seventeenth-century rounded balusters, but was remodelled, probably in this century, and its original site is not known. The house was extended in the nineteenth century, when the facade was rebuilt in brick and the sash windows inserted. There is a large extension to the south, its roof parallel to the main block, and a further extension of one bay to the west perhaps of the late seventeenth century.

In the Middle Ages the Manor of Littleton was held by the Prior of St. Swithun's, and in a lease of 1480 the Prior granted the manor (with responsibility for upkeep of the buildings, type unspecified) to John Smyth for forty years (Greatrex 1978, 135). In the 15th century, ecclesiastical landlords were leasing their manors to farm thus providing great opportunities for peasant farmers to acquire wealth. It is possible that Smyth built the house on the profits of the farm, and the lease specifically states that he will be allowed timber from a designated section of the Lord's woods which he will have to transport to the manor at his own expense (Greatrex 1978, 136). John Smyth died in 1505 and his memorial brass, in itself an indication of his wealth, is in Littleton Church.

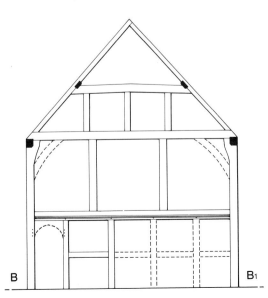

B   B1

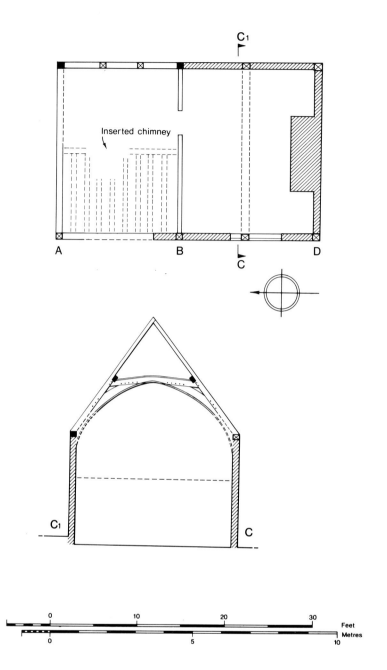

Inserted chimney

A   B   D

C₁

C

0   10   20   30   Feet
0   5   10   Metres

20

Holbrook, Cheriton

Grid Ref: SU 583285

A two-bay hall with at least one further bay c. 1500

Holbrook from the east. (EVR)

This house stands back about 10 yards from a lane beside the village green. Some timber framing with large, curved braces survives on the eastern elevation. The roof is now tiled but was thatched within living memory.

There is a two-bay hall. The hall truss has neatly chamfered arch braces, a cambered collar chamfered on both upper and lower edges, and principal rafters chamfered up to the clasped purlins (cross section C/C'). The hall rafters are heavily smoke blackened.

The roof is half-hipped over the northern bay (A-B) and there are curved wind braces both in this bay and in the hall.

The floored bay A-B has flat joists of medieval type, housed in a spine beam. It is probable that these joists were originally placed axially in medieval fashion, but were sawn through and re-aligned when a chimney and staircase were inserted in this bay.

The hall has been floored and a chimney and brick wall have been built at its southern end. This wall may represent the end of the original house. In the early 19th century an extension was built on the northern end of the house and the western elevation completely rebuilt in brick.

21

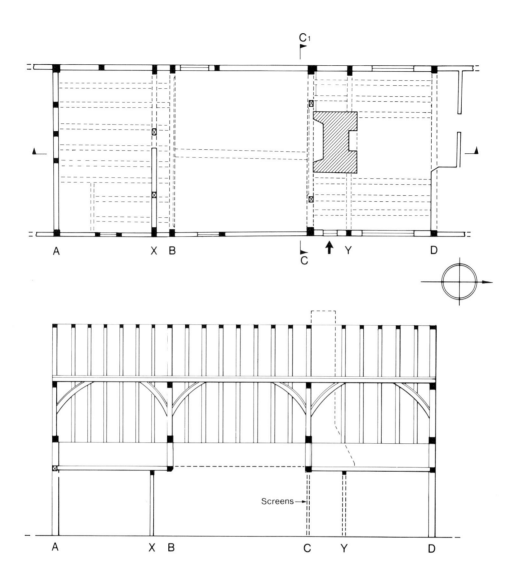

Screens →

A   X   B   C   Y   D

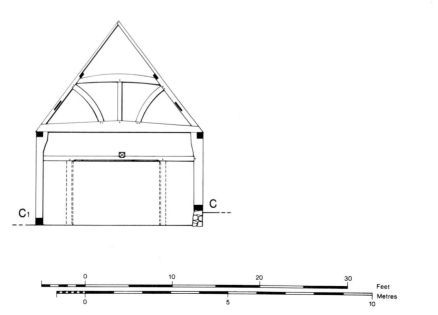

0	10	20	30

Feet
Metres

0   5   10

21

Garden Cottage, West Meon

Grid Ref: SU 641237

A three-bay house with one-bay hall and an internal jetty c. 1450.

The house stands rather apart from the main village centre of West Meon suggesting that it was originally surrounded by its own land and farm property. Its plan and boxframe structure form an interesting comparison and contrast with the cruck house at Park View, Tichborne (4), which may well be contemporary.

The hall is of one bay, but made to seem longer by the internal jetty, which projects beyond the parlour wall to form a canopy over the dais end with its bressumer (B/B') chamfered on the hall side. At the north end of the hall (C-C') two mortices in the bressumer indicate studs forming speres on either side; between them the bressumer is chamfered and stopped. Within the north bay was the passage with space in the external wall-framing for two opposing doors, and the remains of (or a replacement for) the bressumer (Y/Y') in the wall separating the service room from the passage. This bressumer runs beneath the ceiling joists in a fashion similar to that at the Barracks, Wickham (7).

The wall framing surviving on the exterior of the house is of interest as it reflects the structure within.

The side girts mark the original floored bays (A-B, C-D), whereas the hall apparently has no side girt. Further, the position of the internal jetty is marked by a vertical stud. There is a possible site for a hall window at the west side by the passage door, but apparently no windows to light the first floors at either end. The roof was probably originally thatched as it is today. The pattern of raking struts is similar to 3/4 High Street, Hambledon (9). There are windbraces in all three bays, clasped purlins and diminished principals.

Later alterations include the insertion of the chimney into the passage, the flooring of the hall with a spine beam and transverse joists, and the construction of a new staircase in the hall with the abandonment of the staircase in the parlour. The house was extended in timber frame both at the north end and at the south, probably all between c.1600-1650.

The builders of the new church at West Meon were billeted here in 1843-46 and the kitchen window has four panes of yellow glass engraved with lively depictions of Content, Industry, Confidence and Skill.

Garden cottage from the east. The brace marks the post of the
medieval house, which has been extended at each end. (PMJC)

Facing page:
Garden Cottage from the south west

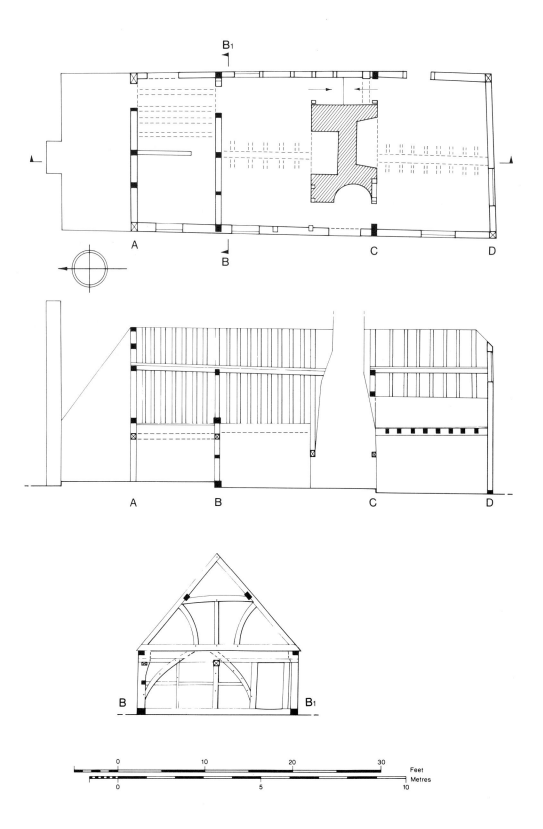

B1

A   B   C   D

A   B   C   D

B   B1

0   10   20   30   Feet
0   5   10   Metres

22

Stoneacre (Blackhouse) Denmead

Grid Ref: SU 663125
A three-bay house with one-bay hall c.1450.

This building is one of the few scattered houses surviving from medieval Denmead. Bay A-B has substantial curved braces on the west elevation rising from low down on the posts to even more substantial wall plates. Similar braces occur in the crossframe B/B' which has a bressumer below the tie beam. This bressumer serves as a doorhead and houses the joists from bay A-B. This arrangement allows greater headroom in the loft-space, as at Garden Cottage (21), and in this way is superior to houses such as Park View (4) where the loft floor is at tie beam level. Some of the original flat-laid axial joists are still visible in bay A-B.

It is probable that all three bays A-D formed the original house and that bay B-C was the hall from the beginning; while bay C-D, though later rebuilt, may represent the original parlour. It is possible, however, that bay A-B was part of an earlier building, since it appears to have heavier scantlings than the rest of the house.

The roof has clasped purlins, curved raking struts and signs of windbraces over the hall (B-C), which are hidden by modern insulation. A gablet survives in truss A/A' and the roof timbers of bays A-B and B-C are heavily smoked. Here, as in neighbouring houses, the lowest layer of thatching is of hops.

The next phase involved flooring over the hall with a spine beam and the insertion of a brick chimney. The south bay, C-D was completely rebuilt sometime in the 17th century, first in timber and later in brick. The impressive wooden ogee doorhead in line with the chimney is, on photographic evidence, a 20th century insertion.

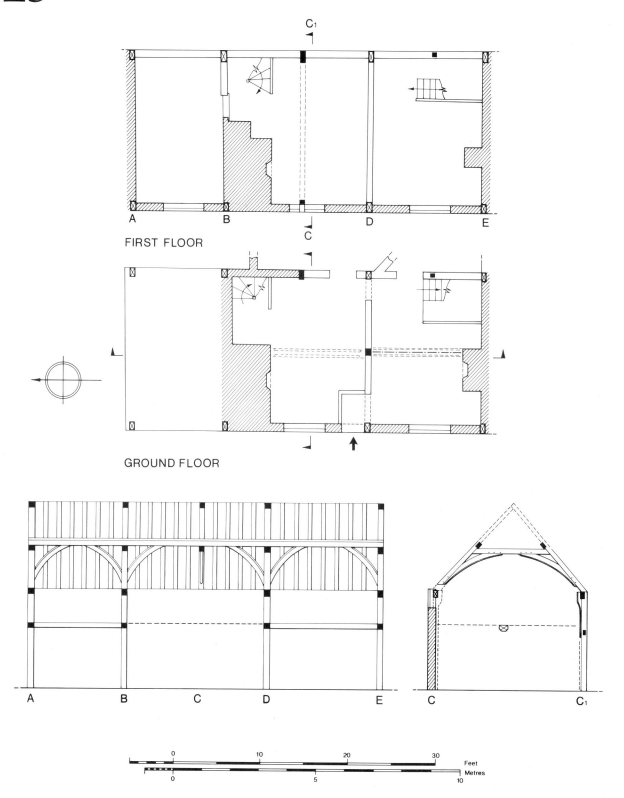

C₁

FIRST FLOOR

GROUND FLOOR

A   B   C   D   E   C   C₁

0   10   20   30   Feet
0   5   10   Metres

23
78 Hursley Village
Grid Ref: SU 428252

A four-bay house with a two-bay hall, c.1520.

The Hursley Post Office and no. 78 together make up the medieval hall house, now concealed behind brick and tile hanging. (JRB)

The house stands lengthways to the main village street and on the east side of it. The two-bay hall might argue for a relatively early date. However, the hall truss is extremely simply finished, with an awkward relationship between principal rafter and wall plate giving a rather unsophisticated impression characteristic of halls of later date or lower status. Little of the wall framing is visible except at the back, where there are simple square panels.

The hall occupies the middle two bays (B-C, C-D), and the present entrance from the street may well be in its original position – indeed it is possible that the timber partition round it represents part of the screens passage. The floored service bay D-E at the south end was divided along the spine beam into two rooms. The roof has clasped purlins and straight collars with straight queen struts in the closed trusses. The hall roof is well blackened. There are wind braces in all bays.

The chimney in the hall seems to have been inserted quite late, perhaps in the eighteenth century. The heavily moulded beam in the hall was brought from elsewhere when the hall was floored. In the nineteenth century the roof was raised and the facade tile-hung on the upper floor and underbuilt with brick on the ground floor. The village post office now occupies the parlour bay on the ground floor and little of the joist arrangement can be seen.

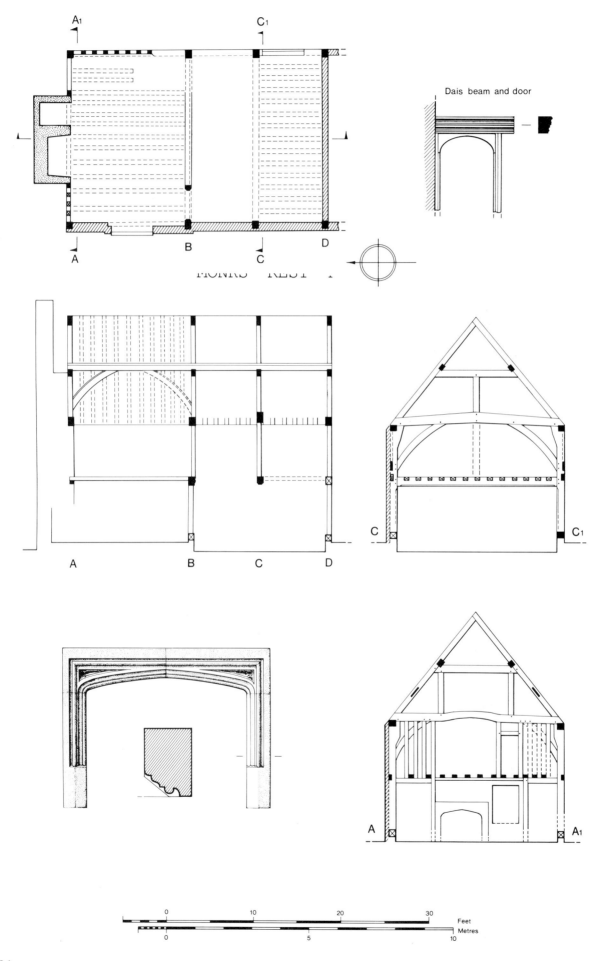

Dais beam and door

MONKS REST

24
Monks Rest, Littleton

Grid Ref: SU 454328
A possible priest's house of three bays. c.1500

This house stands at the eastern edge of the churchyard. It is now tiled and mainly brickclad, but the wall at the north end has close studding and a large external chimney built in a chequerwork pattern of flint and stone. The northernmost bay (A-B) is the parlour with a chamber above. The parlour retains its original axial joists laid flat and a moulded stone fireplace with four-centred arch and simple tracery in the spandrels. The chimney here must be an original feature, since the close studding on the north wall is built up to it and there are no mortices for studs on the tie beam at A/A' where it crosses the chimney. The chimney stack incorporates on the east side a small two-storey

The parlour fireplace at Monks Rest. (PMJC)

compartment under a sloping roof which now forms a closet on each floor but may originally have been a first floor garderobe. The hall bay and the southern service bay are both about 7 feet in length. The bressumer separating the hall from the service bay on the south has no mortices in its soffit, implying that the one-bay hall open to the roof was not separated, unless by a free-standing screen, from its floored service area.

The flooring of this service bay has an inserted spine beam and transverse joists, but mortices remain on the bressumer at C/C' for original axial joists matching those in the parlour and it is these originals which are indicated on the plan.

At the parlour end of the hall is a partly damaged, moulded dais beam of some quality (fig. 5), below which is a doorway with a two-centred arch. The roof is gabled at both ends and has clasped purlins and undiminished principals. One windbrace is visible over the parlour bay but others may be obscured. A central strut rises from tie to collar on either side of the hall, the cross frames of which are heavily sooted.

The hall plan presents serious difficulties in interpretation, since it would seem improbable that a good quality dais beam should be placed so close to an open fire. This raises the possibility that there has been considerable rebuilding in the hall and service bays, although tie beams and roof timbers seem to be consistently integral with the parlour bay. The relatively small chamfer on the bressumer at C/C' may indicate that it is later in date than the original building.

In the Middle Ages, Littleton was a possession of the Priory of St. Swithun's at Winchester and the house has been identified with a retreat for the monks of St. Swithun's which is mentioned in 1500-01 (VCH. Hants.iii,422). A local tradition suggests that this was a priest's house. Its small size, combined with the fine moulded dais beam and heated parlour, would support this suggestion.

25

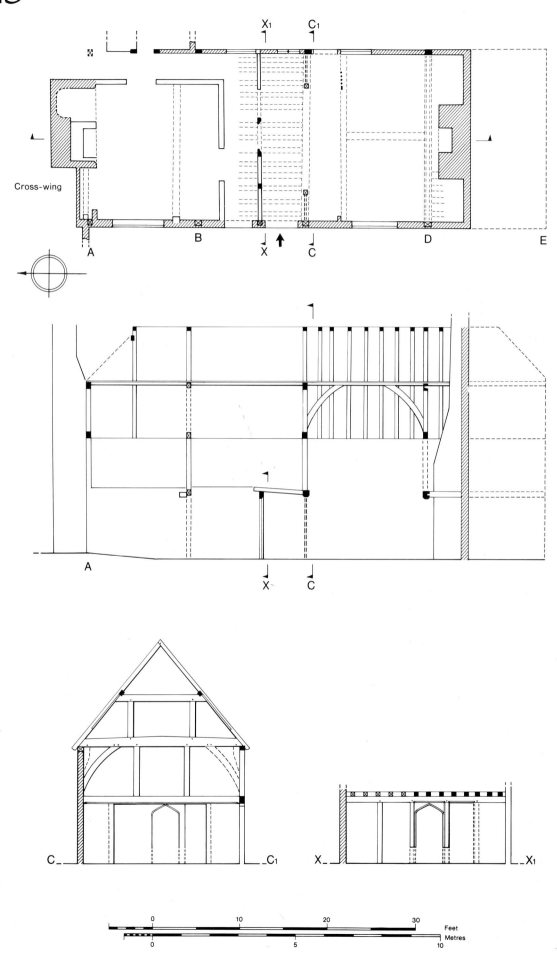

Cross-wing

X₁   C₁

A   B   X   C   D   E

A

X   C

C ___   ___ C₁   X ___   ___ X₁

0   10   20   30   Feet
0   5   10   Metres

98

25
Preshaw Farm Cottages, Preshaw
Grid Ref: SU 568220

A house of four bays with a half-floored hall and overshot passage c. 1480.

Preshaw Farm Cottages from the north-west, showing the added seventeenth century cross wing. (EVR)

The house stands in its own plot in an isolated position within the scattered hamlet of Preshaw.

Although the roof and first floor have been altered at the north end, and half a bay destroyed at the south, enough remains to show that originally this house was of four bays. The hall was apparently of two bays, one being open to the roof with windbraces, and the other floored. This created a half-floored hall as we have seen at Monk's Rest (24) and in a different form at Riverside (2). The floored bay of the hall (D-E) has been partially demolished, but the bressumer (D/D') is chamfered on both sides, its soffit bears no mortices for a partition at ground floor level and there are voided mortices in the southern face of bressumer (D/D') for the axial joists which originally floored bay D-E.

At the north end of the hall (section C/C') the mortices for the spere partition can be seen in the soffit of the bressumer. The passage is overshot by the chamber above. The partition (X/X') between the passage and the service room has two doorways, both with chamfered heads and jambs, and one with a moulded door head. The ceiling joists of the service have been taken out, but the evidence of two doorways would suggest it was divided. The fourth bay to the north is simply built and there is sooting on truss A/A' and on the small gablet, suggesting that bay A-B may have been open. The possibility of this being a brewhouse or even an integral kitchen should be considered, but it is unfortunate that relevant evidence was destroyed when the internal framing was altered, probably in the seventeenth century. At this time a new parlour cross wing (not shown in the drawing) was built on the north end, superseding the original parlour at the south end and effectively reorganising the functions of the rooms.

The roof has clasped purlins, undiminished principals, and straight queen struts. It was half-hipped at the north end. The framing on the west side gives some indication of the position of the windows and rear door.

Later alterations were many and complex and included the insertions of chimney stacks, a kitchen stack in bay A-B, and a smaller one in the truncated bay D-E. There was either a timber or a brick chimney inserted at the north end of the hall together with a new bressumer. No trace of this chimney survives except for some burning on the bressumer.

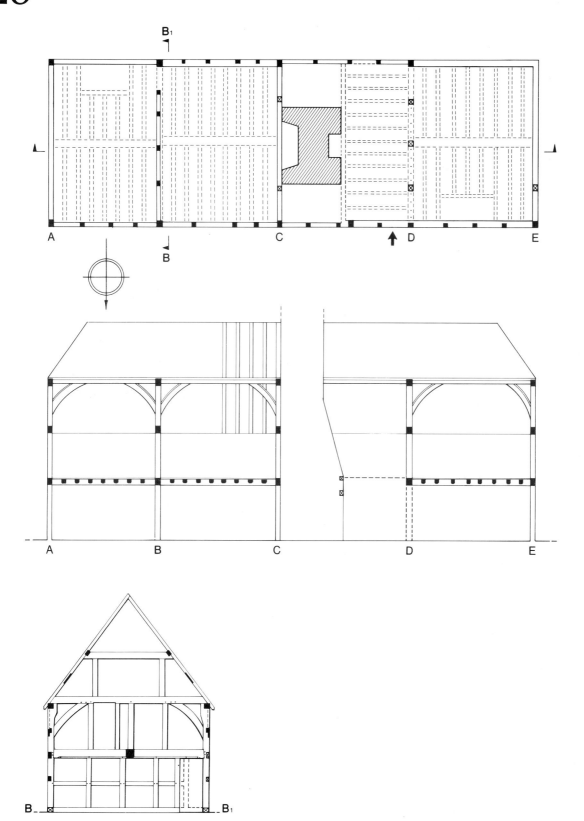

B₁

B

A   C   D   E

A   B   C   D   E

B   B₁

0   10   20   30
Feet
Metres
0   5   10

26

Cottages off Church Lane, Martyr Worthy

Grid Ref: SU 516327

A four-bay house with three floored bays. c. 1550.

The framing of this four-roomed house at Martyr Worthy sets up
a regular rhythm of rails, studs and braces. (PMJC)

This house is set in a large plot and lies parallel to a track which leads from Church Lane towards the hamlet of Chilland. The framing of the north elevation is well preserved, with vestiges of a first floor oriel window. There is a side girt and mid-rails on both floors, creating the small and regular panels that became common in the post-medieval period. The roof is thatched and was half-hipped at both ends. It has clasped purlins and curved wind braces. There are curved braces from principal posts to both tie beams and wall plates.

The hall bay (C-D) is 14ft. 6ins. long and had soot blackening on the tie beams and upper cross frames before recent renovations. It was a one-bay hall, but on the ground floor it may only have been separated from bay B-C by screens. Certainly the evidence of the pegholes in the face of the bressumer at C/C' is consistent with a partially screened opening between hall and parlour, similar to the arrangement at Riverside, East Meon (2).

There are three floored bays. The chamfers on the

joists in bay A-B are of relatively poor quality and this bay measures only 11ft 9ins in length. It was thus probably a service bay. Bays B-C and D-E have relatively well chamfered joists and both measure 13ft. 6ins. in length. Each floored bay has an axial spine beam and transverse joists; a typically post-medieval feature, yet clearly integral to the original building.

The north elevation of bay C-D appears to have been altered and we are tentative about this part of our exterior reconstruction. A chimney was inserted at the east end of the hall and the rest of the hall was floored, probably in the seventeenth century. Perhaps at the same time, the ground floor wall between the hall and bay D-E was removed.

In c.1600, the house was extended by a bay and a half to the west, possibly in order to create a dower house. This extension is timber-framed, although it is slightly later in style than the original house (for example the braces are straight and not curved).

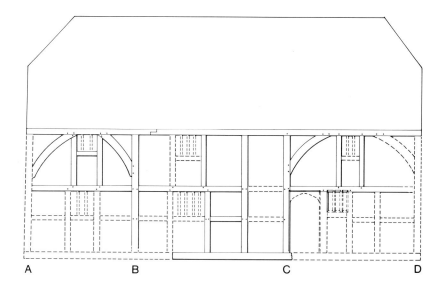

0   10   20   30
Feet
Metres
0   5   10

27

Stapleford Farm, near Durley
Grid Ref: SU 512159

A hall house of three bays c.1500

Mr and Mrs West and their daughter outside Stapleford Farm about 1890. (JRB)

This house lies back some 20 yards from a country lane and near the scattered village of Durley. It has a central, one-bay hall with floored bays on either side. The service bay C-D contains an overshot cross passage.

The best preserved framing is in the north elevation which was stripped in 1983, allowing detailed inspection. Both the door which gave access to the cross passage and the small window beside it had chamfered jambs and heads. This refinement was no doubt intended to impress those entering the house. Elsewhere, the plain timbers form small panels below the side girt, with larger panels above. The end bays have curved braces, and windows with two mullions light each floor.

The roof is half-hipped at both ends and the rafters and cross frames at either end of the hall are heavily smoke-blackened.

The post immediately to the east of C on the northern elevation may be an early insertion, possibly for a smoke bay, and midrails were inserted between sidegirt and wallplate, perhaps in the early 17th century. At about the same time a chimney was inserted in the cross passage, creating a lobby entrance.

28

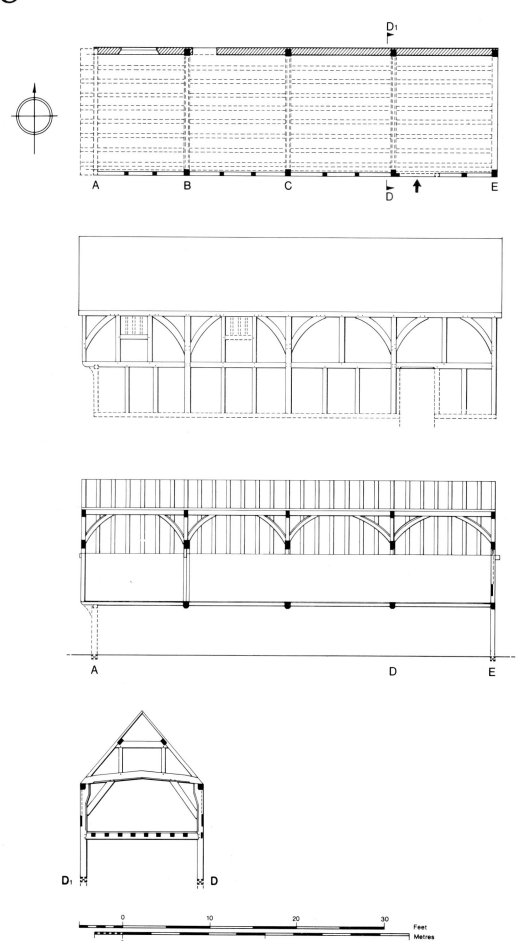

A   B   C   D   E

D₁

A   D   E

D₁   D

Feet

Metres

0   10   20   30

0   5   10

28
81-82 Hursley
Grid Ref: SU 428252

A four-bay, two storeyed building possibly a courthouse, c. 1490-1560

The four regular bays of the possible court house at Hursley. The ground floor entrance was in the nearest bay. (HC)

A four-bay timber framed building set in a plot behind the village street. It is non-domestic in character, having neither a contemporary chimney stack nor an open hearth and hall. The disposition of rooms is also unusual. On the ground floor there are four bays which are open to the full length of the building, forming one long room floored throughout with no opening for stairs. There is a three foot-wide doorway with an inscription "I H John Sm(ith) THE 20 DAY OF IVN 1666" carved on the side girt. There are no windows on the south side. On the north side the posts remain but the evidence for walling is obscured, leaving the possibility that this side was open.

On the first floor, the three bays at the east end are not partitioned and form one long room. Truss B/B' is closed, but there is a central opening for a door. The west end of the building was originally jettied over the ground floor, but the posts have not survived on

the ground floor and it was underbuilt when an end stack was added, perhaps in the eighteenth century. The first floor was lit by two windows on the south side. At the east end there is an opening cut into the tie beam with mortices in the soffit for studs each side, the arrises of the opening being chamfered. This could be either for a doorway or for a large end window – at present this cannot be established because the bricks of the inserted chimney conceal the underside of the beam, where one would expect evidence, if any, of window mullions. We incline, however, to the view that this was a doorway giving access to outside steps, since neither the joists nor the external framing bear evidence of an alternative stair opening.

The roof is of the standard clasped purlin type. All the framing is of good quality, freely chamfered. The bays on the first floor are uniformly eleven feet long. The general impression is of a building

109

The courthouse from the south-east.

carefully constructed to a specific design and for a specific function, which we suggest may have been to serve as a courthouse for the manor of Hursley. Such a courthouse may have become necessary either during the late 15th century when the bishop of Winchester's manor house at Merdon was in decline, or in the 1550's when the bishop surrendered the manor which was then granted to Sir Philip Hoby (Peach 1972, 16-19).

It is difficult to explain the apparent omission of this building from the otherwise very detailed estate map for Hursley of 1588 (IBM) which shows all the occupied houses; but perhaps by this date its use as a courthouse had lapsed and its function been downgraded to agricultural use. Courthouses of similar plan are known; one example at Long Crendon, Bucks, has a large open first floor room with a private room leading off it. A similar arrangement exists at Long Cleavering, Essex, which has been suggested as a Guildhall and at Elstow Moot hall, which, however, had shops on the ground floor (Rigold 1956, 2; Rigold 1968, 1-22).

By the late eighteenth century the building had been converted into two cottages, with brick end chimney stacks, and two staircases. The ground floor of the north side was faced in brick, with the first floor and the whole of the south side tile hung.

29

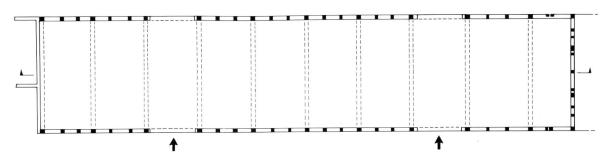

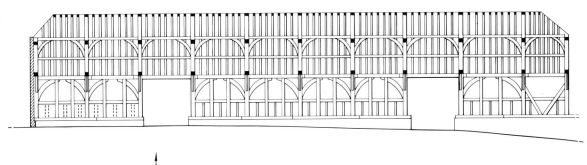

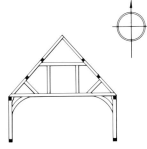

0   20   40   60   Feet
0   10   20   Metres

29

Barn at Webbs Land Farm, Wickham

Grid Ref: SU 562 109

A ten-bay unaisled barn, c1550.

Webb's Land Farm Barn from the south east. The attached pig styes and the granary on staddle stones are later features of the farm yard.

The barn is set along the north side of the farm yard. The land on which it stands slopes down to the east, and there is a brick plinth which supports the timber sill.

The barn is of ten bays with two entrance bays providing threshing floors and access for unloading and stacking the cereal crop from waggons. There are two storage bays on each side of the entrance bays, making a bay rhythm of two storage bays; entrance bay; two storage bays; two storage bays; entrance bay; two storage bays. Each storage bay had a capacity of 2880 cu.ft., making a total of 23040 cu.ft. for the barn (taking the stack up to tie beam level only).

The four waggon doorways are shown on the plan. On the north side, the plate above each door has three mortices. It is difficult to see what these indicate, as there are no corresponding holes in the posts for doorheads, or projecting porches. No original flooring for threshing survives in the waggon bays which are now concreted.

The brick wall at the west end appears to be original. There are two posts half embedded in it, and no signs (such as mortices in the ties) of a timber framed wall that could have preceded it. It is possible the brick wall represents a shortening of an even longer building but this seems unlikely. The bricks are 2" thick, loosely laid like the footings, with a 12" plinth.

The roof is tiled and half hipped at both ends. The roof trusses are uniform except for the alterations at the east end. Each original truss has two tiers of side purlins, the top ones butted to the principals above

the collar, which is supported by two straight studs standing on the tie beam. There are short raking braces from tie to principal, and windbraces morticed into the lower purlins. The framing of the elevations is unusual in its completeness. Each bay has a side girt and curved braces to the plate set to be visible on the outside of the wall. The plate is made up in sections as long as each bay. Some of the exterior cladding survives in the south wall; it is composed of 1/2" planks 8" wide, untapered, set horizontally and overlapping.

The arrangement of the framing is very similar to Sussex barns of the period before the seventeenth century, which are designed for horizontal cladding only on the lower part of the wall up to the mid rail. The small intermediate studs (which are not pegged in and so may be later) support the planking. In Sussex unaisled barns are most common in the fifteenth and sixteenth century but tension bracing is favoured over arch bracing, the more usual Hampshire type. A good parallel to Webbs Land barn is Parsonage farm at Salehurst, Sussex, dated 1550, an unaisled barn of nine bays with two waggon bays (Martin 1977-87 i 12).

In the nineteenth century there was a range of single story timber pens on the west side, and on the south a row of pig sties with a lean-to on the east (Wickham tithe map 1840). Later alterations to the barn include the rebuilding of the eastern bay with straight raking braces, and the insertion of windows into the north side.

This barn was measured by the Solent branch and the Meon Valley branch of NADFAS, and it was drawn by Col. J. Collins.

112

30

A possible sheephouse in mid Hampshire

An open-sided farm building with seven surviving bays, c. 1550

A possible medieval sheephouse, rebuilt and now in use as a barn. (EVR)

This building is part of a farmyard complex on a sub-manor anciently held of the bishops of Winchester. As a manorial building, it is of considerable size and quality.

It seems originally to have been a structure of at least seven bays, without aisles and open along the south side. The roof was gabled at both ends. Five trusses – including a gable end – survive in situ (A-E). The walls were framed at the gable end and on the north side with curved braces and with studs and rails which formed regular panels. There is evidence for this in voided mortices. Stave holes in exterior wall framing show that the walls were infilled with wattle. Hence they were not plank-clad, as was common with 18th century farm buildings in Hampshire.

All trusses have collars with queen struts which rest on what can perhaps best be described as 'upper tie beams'. These rest on queen posts with outfacing jowls and on timbers which function as 'upper wall plates' and which receive arch braces rising from the queen posts (long section). Unfortunately, the assembly joints at this point could not be inspected in detail. The effect is that of a raised aisle, similar to the roof of the demolished building belonging to Oseney Abbey Oxford (Smith, 1958, 118).

The most unusual features of this building are the lower tie beams which, on one side, are cantilevered over the principal posts and inner wall plate to tenon into a flying wall plate. The unmarked soffits of both the inner and flying wall plates argue that this was once an open-sided building, similar to a Devon linhay; although linhays do not seem to have appeared until the 17th century (Thirsk 1961, 750). At least two bays (A-B, B-C) were floored and this feature too is reminiscent of a linhay with its hayloft over the stock shelter beneath. The oversailing or projecting roof on the open, south-eastern side of the building would serve to keep off the rain more effectively, while the open side would allow air to circulate freely. This would be necessary for protecting sheep from diseases to which they are prone in enclosed buildings. Truss B was originally closed from upper collar down to a bressumer at about five feet three inches above the ground, thus making a partition within the loft.

The building has been converted to a barn by removing the side framing along the north wall and adding two aisles. A waggon entrance and threshing floor have been created in the central bay (C-D). The projecting ends of the oversailing tie beams have been supported by the later insertion of oar-shaped props in the south aisle. The ground sills seem to have been cut and swivelled through 90° to form short stubs which cross the aisles. These stubs are

30

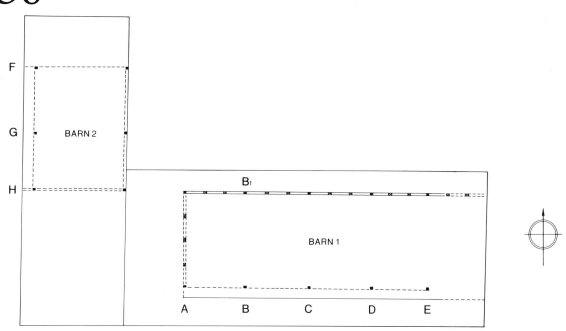

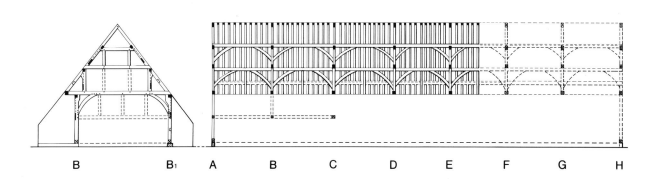

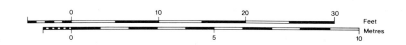

underpinned by low brick plinths, not original, which were possibly inserted to raise the height of the barn and to allow room for a higher waggon entrance.

At right angles to this barn 1 and on the south-west end, is another barn 2 (see plan) incorporating a further three trusses (F-H) including a gable end, which bear a remarkable resemblance to the trusses in barn 1. They comprise oversailing tie beams, flying wall plates and other timbers of exactly the same dimensions as those in barn 1. These timbers

Bishop's Sutton, in 1223-24 a loft or compartment for storing hay was made within the sheephouse (HRO. Eccl. 2 159277) and on the episcopal manor of Farnham, in 1342-43, a sheephouse had joists, presumably for an upper floor (Robo 1935, 124n). Sheephouses continued to be used in the sixteenth century (Thirsk 1961, 187) and there was a sheephouse at Riversdown, near Warnford, Hants, as late as 1663 (HRO. A. Wills 1663 – N. Lorymer).

In the building under discussion the small clearance below the hayloft (about five feet three inches) is

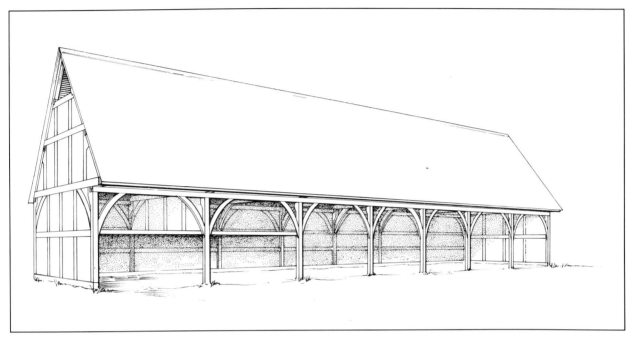

The sheephouse from the south-east.

have been rather crudely re-assembled in barn 2, but they are so unusual that it is difficult to escape the conclusion that they have been re-used from barn 1 and that they were originally attached to bay E-F. (There are no assembly marks visible.) If this is so, then the original structure A to H must have been at least 85 feet in length and about 25 feet high.

As with a linhay, it is possible that this building served the dual purpose of hay storage and stock shelter. There is some reason for believing that the stock in question were sheep and that this was a sheephouse or bercary. In the Hampshire chalklands, great sheephouses were built in the Middle Ages by, for example, the bishops of Winchester. These were properly carpentered timber-framed structures, some of which were almost as expensive to build as great manorial barns. A sheephouse – in Latin *bercaria* – built on the nearby episcopal manor of Old Alresford in 1451-52, contained twelve bays – and had a total length of 150 feet. Its timbers (wall plates, sill beams, etc.) took 14 days to cart to site (HRO. Eccl. 2 159442).

Sheephouses were used for wintering sheep and for storing winter feed in haylofts (Trow-Smith 1957, 158-160: Harvey 1970, 39). On the episcopal manor of

rather too low for cattle and much more suitable for sheep. Furthermore in the sixteenth century sheep were of much greater importance than cattle on this farm. An inventory taken in May 1555, shows that the farm carried 2291 sheep, but only 95 cattle (HRO. B. Wills 1555/78). The farm buildings listed in the inventory were barn, stable, carthouse and 'gornard'. It may be that the building in question had not been made by 1555, or it may have served partly as a gornard, presumably a garner for storing corn or fodder, and as a sheep-house in the winter months when sheep were kept in.

Note: The Latin word used in the medieval pipe rolls of the bishopric of Winchester to denote sheephouse was *'bercaria'*. The standard medieval Latin dictionary translates *'bercaria'* as sheepfold (Latham 1965, 48) which is an enclosure of wattle hurdles. However, it is clear from numerous entries that the writers of the bishopric pipe rolls used *'bercaria'* to denote a substantial timber-framed building. A similar conclusion has been reached in a study of medieval Worcestershire buildings (Field 1965, 121).

Part Four

**Chart summary of the main features
of the houses listed**

Key

✓ = present, surviving evidence
? = probably
S = side
E = end
D = divided (of service bays)
H = heated room
L = later or inserted feature

Notes:

1. Half floored halls are here counted as one bay.

2. Parlour and service bays are only noted where the
   structure of the house clearly indicates a high and
   low end.

3. Ornament here includes mouldings and cusped
   decoration but not simple chamfers.

House number	1	2	3	4	5	6	7	8	9	10	11	12	13	14	15	16	17	18	19	20	21	22	23	24	25	26	27
Approx. date	1350	1350	1350	1450	1450	1450	1450	1450	1450	1350	1400	1480	1380	1470	1550	1425	1430	1375	1500	1500	1450	1450	1520	1500	1480	1550	1500
Cross wing			L														✓								L		
Aisle	✓	✓																									
No. of bays	3	4	2+	4	3	3?	3	3	3	4	2+	3+	3	3	4	4	4+	2+	4	3	3	3	4	3	4	4	3
No. of hall bays (note 1)	2	2	2	2	2	1	1	1	1	2	2	1	1	1	1	2	2	2	2	2	1	1	2	1	1	1?	1
Half floored hall								✓							✓									✓	✓	✓?	
Galleried hall										E?			S	S	S	S	S										
Parlour bay (note 2)													✓			✓			✓		✓		✓	H			✓
Service bay (note 2)													✓			D			✓		✓		D		D		
Passage within service													✓			✓					✓			✓			✓
Wealden							✓	✓	✓		✓																
Jetty							S	S	S	E?			E	S/E	S		S										
Box frame	✓	✓					✓	✓	✓	✓	✓	✓	✓	✓	✓	✓	✓	✓	✓	✓	✓	✓	✓	✓	✓	✓	✓
Base cruck		✓	✓																								
Cruck with ridge					✓	✓																					
Cruck without ridge				✓																							
Common rafter roof	✓	✓	✓							✓			✓														
Crown post										✓	✓	✓															
Side purlins					✓	✓	✓	✓	✓	✓		✓	✓		✓	✓	✓	✓		✓	✓	✓	✓	✓	✓	✓	✓
Arch brace (roof)	✓	✓	✓	✓	✓										✓	✓		✓	✓				✓				
Arch brace (walls)							✓	✓		✓		✓		✓	✓	✓		✓	✓					✓	✓	✓	✓
Tension brace										✓			✓	✓													
Studs only				✓		✓																					
Close studding														✓				✓					✓				
Screens													✓			✓					✓	✓			✓		
Door frame													✓		✓	✓		✓							✓		✓
Window frame				✓									✓			✓										✓	✓
Signs of louvre				✓												✓											
Ornament [3]													✓						✓	✓					✓		
Internal jetty				✓																		✓					
	1	2	3	4	5	6	7	8	9	10	11	12	13	14	15	16	17	18	19	20	21	22	23	24	25	26	27

Gazetteer

Further medieval houses in central Hampshire

31 Ashley Cottage SU 380313
3-bay box framed house, with 1-bay hall that has an internal jetty at upper end indicated by two posts in elevation. Clasped purlin roof.

32 Boarhunt Cottage SU509119
2-bay cruck hall with box framed storeyed bay (Harris 1982, 14)

33 Botley Manor Farm SU 509119
Surviving end frame of hall, integral with 3-bay cross-wing. Truncated side purlins.

34 Chalton The Red Lion SU 731160
Partially aisled wealden with 1-bay hall. Side purlin roof.

35 Compton Drove Cottage SU467256
4-bay box framed with clasped purlin roof. 2-bay hall half floored over. cf. Preshaw Farm Cottages (25)

36 Curdridge Harfields Farm SU 538151
1-bay hall. 16th century cross-wing added.

37 Denmead Rookwood Farm SU 652132
Norman first floor hall of stone rubble with chimney in thickness of n. wall. Close studded timber frame extension to east of c. 1550.

38 Denmead Bittles SU 641136
Service end of wealden house, rebuilt in 17th century. Remnants of timber chimney at lower end of hall.

39 East Meon Hockley Cottage SU 681221
Box framed 4-bay house with clasped purlin roof, smoking indicates 1 bay hall, or possibly a 2-bay half floored hall.

40 East Meon Court House SU 681222
Stone manor house c. 1425 with large hall, service block with chamber above, crown post roofs.

41 Exton No. 2 Grove Cottages SU 613209
Very small 1-bay hall with clasped purlin roof survives between two later cross wings.

42 Exton Mariners Cottage SU613211
3-bay boxframed house wtih clasped purlin roof includes 1-bay hall. Plain door head framed into end of hall.

43 Hambledon Manor Farmhouse SU 646150
Flint and stone Norman building in two blocks. Three roundheaded doorways in s. wall suggest service wing to hall now lost. Roof renewed. c. 1400 with arch braced collar and side purlins with cusped windbraces. Later timber framed north wing has smoke bay at s. end.

44 Hambledon Timbered Cottage, East Street SU 648151
3-bay house with 2-bay hall having inserted central timber chimney. Threaded purlin roof, half-hipped.

45 Hambledon The Green Man SU 643148
2 bays of a cruck house remain including a 1-bay hall. (Lewis 1976)

46 Hambledon Scotland Cottage, Glidden SU 670156
4-bay box framed house with 2-bay hall having arch-braced collar, clasped purlins, diminished principals.

47 Hambledon Teglease Farm, Chidden SU 654186
2-bay house, 1-bay hall and other bay with cross-passage and services. Clasped purlin roof.

48 Headbourne Old Rectory Worthy SU 485322
3-bay house including 1-bay hall. Added 16th century cross-wing.

49 Kingsworthy Old Cottage SU 49432
Roof remnants of 2 bays of a cruck building.

50 Littleton Red House SU 453329
2-bay house with 1-bay hall. Clasped purlin roof. Large curved braces in N. elevation.

51 Littleton The White House SU455325
4-bay house with evidence of at least one open bay. Clasped purlin roof with wind braces.

52 Lomer Lomer Farmhouse SU 590236
3-bay house with 1-bay hall and with cross passage. (Collins and Oliver 1971, 67-76).

53 Meonstoke   Cottages   SU 611202
3-bay timber framed house with central 1-bay hall.

54 Micheldever Old Forge   SU 515390
3-bay box framed house with half-floored hall.

55 Micheldever Barn Cottage   SU 513392
Box framed with parlour bay and 1- or 2-bay hall. 16th century cross-wing at parlour end.

56 Owslebury   Marwell Hall   SU 508216
4 pairs of base crucks to large open hall of 3 bays. Stone cross-wings added later. (Crook 1987b, 15-17)

57 Petersfield   Tully's   SU 744231
The Spain
Service bay and 2-bay hall of Wealden. Clasped purlin roof, arch braced collar to hall truss. (Petersfield Historical Society)

58 Petersfield   48 College Street   SU 748236
2-bay box framed house including 1-bay hall. Very simple crown post roof. (Petersfield Historical Society)

59 Pitt   Oddicombe   SU 451280
3-bay cruck house with 1-bay hall between 2 pairs of crucks. 16th century cross wing.

60 St. Cross   Back Street   SU 477280
Box framed house with hall and service in single bays, and parlour in cross wing. Added lateral stack.

61 Soberton   Ingoldfield Farm   SU 613144
3-bay box framed house with 2-bay hall having plain arch braced collar. Clasped purlin roof. Added 16th century wing.

62 Soberton   St Clair's Farm
Stone-built 2-storey block.   **SU604154**

63 Southwick   30 West Street   SU 625085
3-bay box framed with 2-bay hall having arch braced collar. Clasped purlin roof with flat-laid common rafters and diminished principals.

64 Tichborne   Sevington Farm   SU 575296
Box framed house. Vestiges of late medieval house at right angles to well-preserved extension of c. 1600.

65 Titchfield   7 and 9 Church   SU 541058
Street
3-bay box-framed house with 1-bay hall. Side purlin roof with curved queen struts.

66 Stoke   Old Keepers   SU 486393
Charity   Cottage
Cruck house with floored bay and 1-bay of 2-bay hall. Hall truss with arch braces (apex C). smoke bay.

67 Twyford   Cottage   SU 481244
2 bays of cruck building

68 Upper   Park Cottage   SU 581176
Swanmore
Cruck House with 1-bay hall and a floored bay, rebuilt c. 1600 and later.

69 Upper Wield Rose Cottage   SU 629387
3-bay house with single bay hall. Clasped purlin roof.

70 Warnford   Riversdown   SU 603247
2-bay hall with base cruck and aisled cross-frame with service doors.

71 Warnford   King John's House   SU 623226
Early 13th C. ruined stone – built aisled hall with service block. (Nesbitt 1906, 299)

72 Wickham   Dale Cottage,   SU 573115
Bridge Street
3-bay box-framed house with 1-bay hall. Clasped purlin roof.

73 Winchester   36 Middle Brook   SU 483296
Street
3-bay box-framed house with parlour end jettied onto street, side-passage, 1-bay hall with 1 original and 1 inserted gallery. (Keene, 1985 158, 736-8)

74 Winchester   Pilgrim's School   SU 482291
and Hall
Apparently 2 quasi-aisled halls, 1 hall with hammerbeam roof, the other with 1 pair base crucks. (Crook 1982, 85-101)

75 Winchester   Godbegot   SU48295
Block of urban tenements with galleried single bay halls. (Keene 1985, 491)

76 Ampfield   Ratlake   SU416235
Fragments of a cruck building reused in a 17c farmhouse. Includes a moulded dais beam c. 1450 (fig. 4)

77 Littleton   St. Swithun's CottageSU 455325
3-bay house with one bay hall. Clasped purlin roof.

Glossary

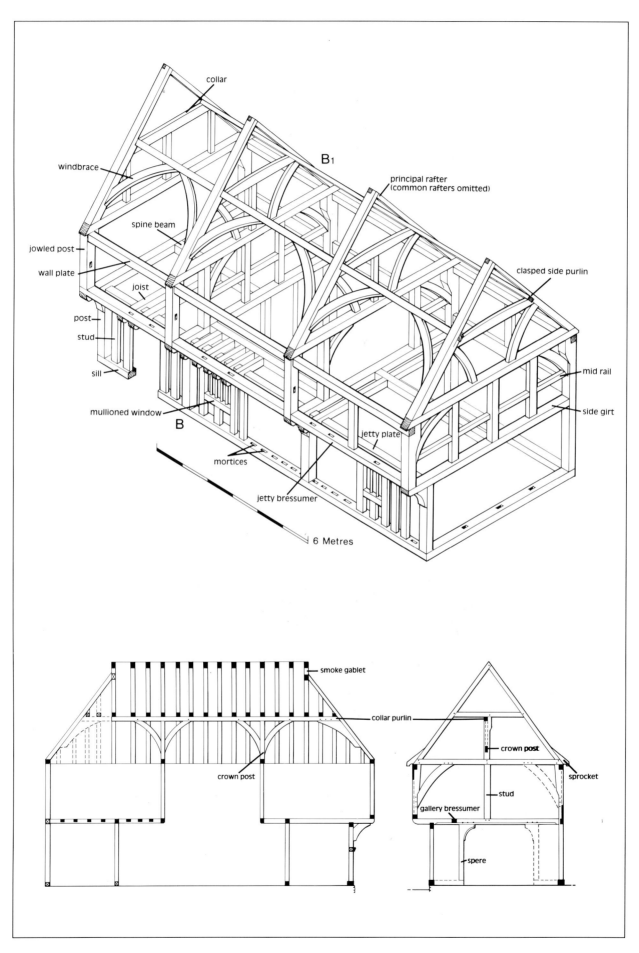

collar

B₁

windbrace

principal rafter
(common rafters omitted)

spine beam

jowled post

clasped side purlin

wall plate

joist

post

stud

mid rail

sill

side girt

mullioned window

B

jetty plate

mortices

jetty bressumer

6 Metres

smoke gablet

collar purlin

crown post

crown post

sprocket

stud

gallery bressumer

spere

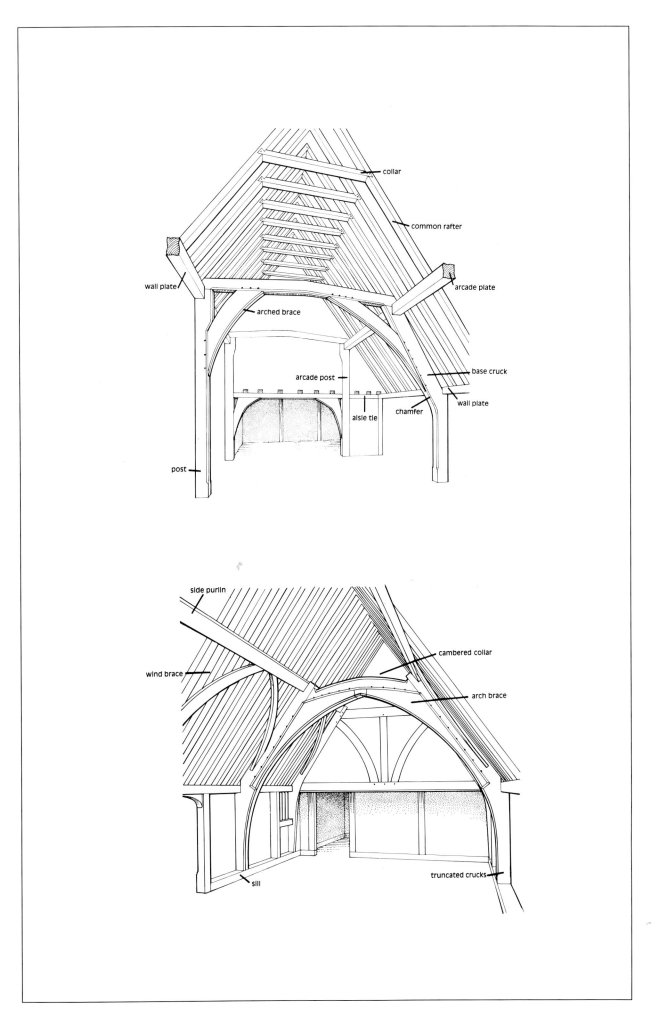

collar

common rafter

wall plate

arcade plate

arched brace

arcade post

base cruck

wall plate

aisle tie

chamfer

post

side purlin

cambered collar

wind brace

arch brace

sill

truncated crucks

123

Bibliography

Primary Sources

HRO Hampshire Record Office, Southgate St., Winchester
A wills, Archdeaconry wills
B wills, Bishopric wills
U wills, Unclassified wills.

Eccl 2 159277, The pipe roll of the bishopric of Winchester, 1223-24.
Eccl 2 159442, The pipe roll of the bishopric of winchester, 1451-52.
Eccl 155651, Survey of the manor of Cheriton c.1560.
Eccl 158819: 6/10, Survey of the manor of Hambledon c.1560.
Eccl 2 158819: 10/10, Rental of the manor of Bishop's Waltham 1464.

PWCM Photographs in Winchester City Museum, 75 Hyde Street. Negative number is given.

IBM A survey of the Manor of Merdon dated 1588 by Ralph Tieswell (thought to have been redrawn in 1700).

Printed and Secondary Sources

Alcock, N.W. 1981
Cruck Construction, an introduction and catalogue. C.B.A. Reasearch Report 42.

Alcock, N.W. and Moran, M. 1984
Low open-truss beams (Mantel Beams) Problems of functions and distribution. Vernacular Architecture 15.

Baggs, A.P. 1967
Hook Farm, Lower Woodcott, Hants. Transactions of the Newbury and District Field Club XI no.4.

Barley, M. 1961
The English Farmhouse and Cottage. London.

Barley, M. 1967
Rural Housing in England, in Thirsk, J. (ed.) The Agrarian History of England and Wales 1500-1640. Cambridge.

Beresford, M. 1959
Six New Towns of the Bishops of Winchester 1200-1255. Medieval Archaeology III.

Collins, F. and Oliver, J. 1971
Lomer: a study of a deserted medieval village. Proceedings of the Hampshire Field Club XXVIII.

Crook, P.M.J. 1982
The Pilgrims' Hall, Winchester. Proceedings of the Hampshire Field Club and Archaeological Society 38.

Crook, P.M.J. 1987a
Winchester Cathedral Deanery. Proceedings of the Hampshire Field Club 43.

Crook, P.M.J. 1987a
Marwell's medieval roof. Hampshire Field Club and Archaeological Society Newsletter. New Series no. 8.

Currie, C.R. and Fletcher, J.M. 1972
Two early cruck houses in North Berkshire identified by radio carbon. Medieval Archaeoogy 16.

Faulkener, P.A. 1975
The Surviving Medieval Buildings in Platt, Colin (ed). Excavations in Medieval Southampton. Leicester.

Field, R.K. 1965
Worcestershire Peasant Buildings. Household Goods and Farming Equipment in the Later Middle Ages. Medieval Archaeology IX

Fletcher, J.M. 1981
Tree Ring Dates for Buildings with Oak Timber . Vernacular Architecture 12.

Fletcher, J.M. and Crook, P.M.J. 1984
The date of the Pilgrims' Hall, Winchester, Proceedings of the Hampshire Field Club 40.

Forrester, Harry, 1972
Medieval Gothic Mouldings. Chichester.

Gray, P. 1980
Nutfield and Burstow, The history of the landscape and buildings. Caterham.

Greatrex, J. 1978
The Register of the Common Seal. Hampshire C.C.

Harding, J. 1976
Four Centuries of Charlwood Houses. Charlwood, Surrey.

Harding, J. 1980
Medieval vernacular roof trusses in Surrey. Vernacular Architecture II.

Hare, J. (forthcoming)
Bishop's Waltham Palace... Archaeological Journal.

Harris, R. ed. 1982
Guide to the Wealden and Downland Museum , Singleton.

Harries, J. 1986
Crondall in the Time of Elizabeth I. Farnham & District Museum Society.

Harvey, N. 1970
A History of Farm Buildings in England and Wales. Newton Abbott.

Hayter, Sir W. 1970
William of Wykeham, Patron of the Arts. London.

Hewett, C.A. 1980
English Historic Carpentry. Chichester.

Hoskins, W.G. 1963
Provincial England. London

Keene, D. 1985
A Survey of Medieval Winchester. Winchester Studies 2 vols. Oxford.

Latham, R.D. 1965
A revised Medieval Latin word-list. London.

Lewis, E.R. 1976
Hampshire Crucks, Hampshire Field Club Newsletter 2.

Lewis, E.R. 1979
A Jettied House at Wickham, Hampshire. Proceedings of the Hampshire Field Club 36.

Lloyd, N. 1931
A History of the English House. London.

Martin, D. & B. 1977-87
Historic Buildings in Eastern Sussex. 4 vols. Robertsbridge.

Mason, R.T. 1957
Fourteenth Century Halls in Sussex. Sussex Archaeological Collections 95.

Mason, R.T. 1958
Four single bay halls. Sussex Archaeological Collections 96.

Mason, R.T. 1969
Framed Buildings of the Weald. Horsham.

Meirion-Jones, G.I., and others 1987
The Dating by dendrochronology of three Northamptonshire Halls. Vernacular Architecture 18.

Mercer, E. 1975
English Vernacular Houses. HMSO.

Mercer, E. 1985
The Roof of the Palace Stables. in Lewis, E. Excavations in Bishops Waltham. Proceedings of the Hampshire Field Club and Archaeological Society 41.

Moore, J.S. 1985
Probate Inventories: Problems and Prospects. in Riden, P. (ed.).

Nesbitt, N.C.H. 1906
Notes on a Ruined Building in Warnford Park. Proceedings of the Hampshire Field and Archaeological Society V.

Peach, D.L. 1972
The History of Hursley Park. Hursley (IBM UK).

Pevsner, N. and Lloyd, D. 1967
Hampshire and the Isle of Wight. London.

Portman, D. 1974
Vernacular Architecture in the Oxford Region in the sixteenth and seventeenth centuries in Chalklin, C.W. and Havinden, M.A. Rural Change and Urban Growth 1500-1800. London.

Priestley, U. Corfield, P.J. and Sutermeister, H. 1982
Rooms and room use in Norwich housing, 1580–1730. Post-Medieval Archaeology 16.

RCHME 1980
Ancient and Historical Monuments in the City of Salisbury vol I. London HMSO.

Riden, P. (ed.) 1985
Probate Records and the Local Community, Gloucester.

Rigold, S.E. 1956
The Moot Hall, Elstow. Bedfordshire County Council.

Roberts, E. (forthcoming)
Southampton Inventories 1450-1575 Southampton Record Series.

Robo, E. 1935
Medieval Farnham. Farnham.

Short, Philip 1980
The Fourteenth-Century Rows of York. Archaeological Journal 137.

Smith, J.T. 1958
Medieval Roofs, a classification. Archaeological Journal CXV 1958.

Smith, V.F. 1984
Hampshire Inventories at the Public Record Office, London. Hampshire Field Club Newsletter: New Series 2.

Stenning, D.F. 1985
Timber framed shops 1300-1600: comparative plans. Vernacular Architecture 16.

Swain, E.R. 1968
Divided and Galleried Hall Houses. Medieval Archaeology XII.

Thirsk, J. (ed) 1961
Agrarian History of England and Wales 1500-1640 Cambridge.

Trow-Smith R. 1957
A History of British Livestock Husbandry to 1700. London.

V.C.H. Hants 1900-14
The Victoria County History of Hampshire and the Isle of Wight. 5 vols. London.

Warren, W.T. 1903
Winchester Illustrated. Winchester.

Wood, M. 1965
The Medieval English House, London.

A note on dendrochronology

A little while after the completion and typesetting of the text, the opportunity arose to examine two of the buildings described, Park View at Tichborne (4) and The Crease, Micheldever (16) in order to determine their date by dendrochronology. The work was carried out by John Esling of the Tree Ring Dating Laboratory, Nottingham University, whose report is given below.

The results provide the first reasonably 'absolute' dates for the construction of these two buildings. both in the third quarter of the fifteenth century. The estimated filling dates of 1355 for the reused cruck at Tichborne and 1480 for the building itself are particularly interesting (even though tentative) in providing a chronological span for cruck construction in the county. The date for the Crease, Micheldever (estimated felling date 1476) though slightly later than suggested in the text, tends to confirm our suggestion that cruck framed houses and box framed houses were being built at the same time.

It would perhaps be appropriate here to mention a further discovery, that of a firm construction date for East Meon Court House (40) which though of manorial status and not directly comparable to the more ordinary houses described in this book, yet has two good post roofs which can now be dated to 1394-1397 on the documentary evidence of the pipe rolls of the Bishopric of Winchester which itemise all the building work at East Meon in great detail and will be the subject of a separate study in due course.

A report on the samples taken for dendrochronology

A brief survey of tree ring dating

The annual growth, as seen in the widths of the annual rings of oak trees, varies from year to year by amounts largely dependent on the weather conditions during the growing season. Over a relatively long period of time this gives rise to a sequence of annual rings whose pattern of widths, one after the other, is more or less unique for each such period. As a result one piece of timber from a building may be dated relative to another from the same locality if each shows the same or a very similar pattern of ring widths. From a whole series of buildings an extended sequence of ring widths, representing the averages for oak in the locality for the years, can be constructed and a master sequence or chronology formed.

Master chronologies for oak have been formed, for example, for England as a whole, the south of England and the East Midlands, and can be used to date samples from Hampshire. Ultimately it is hoped to construct a sequence for Hampshire covering, say the last 600-700 years, which could then be used to date buildings in the area. The process of comparing sequences of ring widths with one another is called cross-matching.

Most samples are taken by means of coring. The holes are then plugged and carefully disguised. Samples from several timbers in each house are necessary to provide enough data to give statistically acceptable results, and six or more are usually retrieved from each building.

The sequence of ring-widths from these samples are first cross-matched with each other. Usually a group of them match together well and a sequence of average ring widths, one for each year of the period covered is formed. This represents the building as a whole and is called a site sequence. If this has eighty or more rings then dates obtained by cross-matching a site sequence with a master chronology can usually be accepted with confidence.

It is worth pointing out that tree ring dating does not always work for a variety of reasons. The most common problem is that the timbers have very few rings – say less than sixty. Dates for such timbers can sometimes be obtained but they must be treated with some caution. Such dates are useful, for example, for suggesting in which periods to undertake documentary research.

The date obtained by cross matching samples from a house with a master chronology is the date of the last ring on the sample. If bark is present on a dated timber then the felling date is known. If no bark is present an estimate of the felling date can often be suggested. This is because the outer thirty or so rings (called sapwood rings) of a growing oak which contains the tree's lymphatic system, are markedly lighter in colour than the rest of the trunk, called the heartwood. Sapwood rings are easily recognisable if present. If one or more (say 12) survive on a sample, then by adding on the extra years to make a total of 30 (viz 18), the felling date can be estimated. It is usually the case that some of the timbers in a medieval building will have retained at least some sapwood. Since such buildings were usually constructed of green (unseasoned) timber the estimated felling date of the timber used and the construction date of the house are likely to coincide.

(It is good practice to give a range of felling dates to allow for variation in the number of sapwood rings extant on the tree at felling: 15 to 50 is reasonable and includes 95% of all mature oaks.)

The Crease, Micheldever (16)

Timbers at The Crease, Micheldever were sampled by coring. The building appears to be of a single phase of construction. Eight samples were taken by coring parts of the building that are clearly integral to the structure as it was originally built. Sanding and measuring showed most of the samples to be rather short with a single exception that had eighty rings. Despite initial pessimism and with some work, it proved possible to unite five of the eight samples into a single site sequence of 95 rings. This sequence was cross-matched with various established national chronologies producing an acceptable series of correlations when the date of the first ring is 1370 and that of the last is 1462. Two of the five samples showed clear evidence for the presence of a heartwood/sapwood boundary and two others have intact sapwood, one with a single ring and the other with twenty surviving rings of sapwood. The relative dates of the samples clearly indicated that they had all originated from trees felled at the same time. The average last heartwood ring for the sequence was calculated to represent growth for the year 1446. Using estimates for the number of sapwood rings extant on a living oak tree (see above), it is possible to suggest a felling date range for the timbers sampled. The fact that the longest sample with its twenty sapwood rings has a last ring date of 1462 indicates that the earliest possible felling date is 1463. The end of the felling date range is 1496 (1446+50). The estimated felling date on the basis of the average extent of sapwood on a mature, living oak, is 1476 (1446+30). However, as most of the samples seemed to come from fairly young trees, and timber that produced the sample with twenty sapwood rings showed sign of retaining almost complete sapwood at the point at which the sample was taken, a felling date range in the earlier part of the range suggested above, i.e. 1463 to 1476, is strongly indicated.

Park View Cottage, Tichborne (4)

Eight samples from the house were retrieved by taking cores. A ninth sample was obtained from a rafter that had been removed and stored during the ongoing restoration of the building. These were brought back to the laboratory in the Archaeology Dept at Nottingham University. The building basically appears to be of one phase though one pair of cruck blades had clearly been reused from elsewhere (truss D/D').

Preparation of the samples showed most to have a reasonably good number of rings though there were few sapwood rings still surviving. Analysis by the standard Litton/Zainodin cross-matching and grouping procedure, a computer technique developed at Nottingham, generated a single site sequence of 85 rings formed from two of the samples.

This site sequence was cross-matched with a range of national chronologies that are available on the computer, producing a series of correlations where the date of the first ring is 1368 and that of the last is 1452.

Both samples within the sequence had the remains of sapwood on their outer surfaces. The last heartwood rings on these samples represent growth during the years 1448

and 1452 respectively. The average of these is 1450. This is the average last heartwood ring for the sequence. The estimated felling date range for this site sequence therefore extends from 1465 (1450+15) to 1500 (1450+50). The estimated felling date is 1480 (1450 + 30).

Unfortunately the cross-matches with established national chronologies were not sufficiently good for this date to be accepted with any great confidence. However some of the other individual samples produced similar dates by the same process of cross-matching with national chronologies, and this lends some support to this dating. Despite this the dating suggested should be treated with a good deal of caution. It is, as noted in the brief survey above, a suggestion only.

The single exception is one sample taken from a cruck blade of truss D/D' in the house. This truss has open mortice holes and has clearly been reused from a previous building. This produced its highest levels of correlation when the date of the first ring is 1285 and that of the last is 1335. This sample has ten surviving sapwood rings. Using the method described, the felling date range is 1340-1375 with a suggested felling date of 1355.

However, as this is a single, short sample of just 51 rings dating is, for now, just an interesting suggestion.

Conclusion

These two sites demonstrate the strengths and weaknesses of tree ring dating/dendrochronology. At the first site, tree ring dating produced a short range for the construction of the building, 1463-76. On the other hand for Park View, Tichborne the dating is more tentative.

In the first case the dates suggested gives objective evidence for the date of the building, independent of any assessments based on architectural style or features. In the second instance the dating really should not be relied upon and should be used to suggest further documentary and historical research. It is interesting that the tree ring dates obtained for both cottages are broadly in line with those suggested previously.

John Esling